BEGiNNER WATCHMAKiNG

HOW TO BUILD YOUR VERY FIRST WATCH

BY TIM SWIKE

Please Read This FIRST

Terms of Use

Please send questions or comments to: indyebooks@aol.com

Several trademarks are used in this book for narrative purposes. Each trademark is the property of its respective owners.

Copyright 2010

ISBN-13:
978-1456451653

ISBN-10:
1456451650

This book is dedicated to my family, and my beautiful daughter, Maddie.

TABLE OF CONTENTS

INTRODUCTION

The book, BEGINNER WATCHMAKING, was written to introduce you to the fascinating world of watch making. It is designed for the average lay person with little to no knowledge of watch mechanics, building, or repair. This book will teach you some of the basics on how a watch works. It will also show you how to find the right watch parts, how to assemble them, and how to regulate the time, so that the finished watch runs accurately. In other words, you will be able to build a watch with ease once you learn a few tricks of the trade.

Since this book mainly focuses on watch building and assembling, along with a few simple repairs, you will need to be on the lookout for mechanical or quartz watch movements that are running, or better yet new. If the movements have serious problems, like a broken mainspring or damaged crystal resonator, then you will probably need to take some watch repair classes before attempting to make those repairs. However, one of the nice things about watch repair is that parts are cheap. It is often much easier to just buy a new part, or movement, and install it. For example, you can find high quality Seiko 7S26 automatic movements online for as little as $45, and ETA, Ronda, or Miyota quartz movements online for $10 or less. Even expensive $500 watches often have $10-$30 quartz movements in them. And some of the high end automatic watches that sell for $2000 or more in stores have $130 ETA 2824 movements in them. And although these parts are very high in quality, they are not very expensive to manufacture. So a watch that cost you $200 to build could be worth up to $2000 in a retail store setting. Now you can see why building your own watch might be fun, economical, and even profitable. It's because the mark up on luxury items is usually astronomical!

Let's get back to the subject of watch repairs. Let's say you find a great deal on a used watch on Ebay that is running good, but has a broken crystal, or crown, and it also needs a new dial, or new set of hands? No problem. This book will show you how to make those repairs, which really just involves buying the new parts and installing them. *(Note: some watchmakers actually do fabricate parts for vintage watches that can no longer be purchased, however, that skill involves advanced watch making, which is not discussed in this entry level book).* Crystals, crowns, dials, and hands can be purchased online for a few dollars, and can be installed with little difficulty. You just need to know what size parts to order, and how to install them. Better yet, you don't even need to buy another watch in order to use this book. You can modify the watch you are wearing right now, and make it a one of a kind. Change the color of the hands, or buy a really cool brandless dial and swap out the old one. In just a few minutes you can increase your watch's value by $50 or more.

So now that you have a better idea about what *BEGINNER WATCHMAKING* is about, let's discuss some of the basic watch terms you should know. First of all, what exactly is watch making? Basically, it is the process of building and repairing watches. And watches are devices that measure the time and date. Measuring, or studying time, is a process known as Horology. And if you are into Horology, then you are probably a Horologist. Sounds simple enough, doesn't it?

So exactly how old is the art of Horology, or watch making? Although the exact dates are often guesses at best, one thing is for certain, watch making is pretty old. It is said to have started with the first portable clock, which was designed in Nuremberg, Germany by Peter Henlein in 1504. As far as timekeeping went, this clock was not accurate, and it only had one hand to tell the time with. Second hands wouldn't come into existence until the late 1600's. It has been said that Henlein referred to his clock as his "Nuremberg Egg", but that translation has been theorized by many to be inaccurate. Before the invention of this egg clock, timepieces were not very portable. In fact, they were quite massive and cumbersome mechanical devices, often seen in large towers. B\And before the large clocks existed, water clocks and sundials were used to tell the time, dating as far back as 1400 BC in Egypt. However, the ability to tell time probably goes back even further, dating back to the first civilization. As you can see, timekeeping, just like art, is one of the oldest inventions known to man.

One of the first known clocks to be worn by an individual dates back to the late 15th Century. Back then, small clocks, or clock-like watches were worn on garments, or worn on chains, and were merely thought of as jewelry, since they were pretty inaccurate when it came to telling the time. It wasn't until the 17th Century that these watches had transitioned into somewhat useful timekeeping devices known as pocket watches. Watch makers back then would not only assemble these pocket watches, they would build all of the parts by hand as well. These early pocket watches used clock movements combined with a crown wheel escapement as their main source of power. Although pocket watches back then were popular among men, they were still big and clumsy, and became inaccurate when the mainspring lost maximum tension.

As the design of the pocket watch improved along with the growth of the railroad industry, sales dramatically increased, making the watch a household name. Women, on the other hand, still continued to wear the small pendant watches around their necks or wrists. But not all women wanted to wear a piece of jewelry with a dial and hands on it. Jump ahead to 1812 and you will discover the first known wristwatch, created by the famous Swiss watchmaker, Abraham-Louis Breguet, which was made for Caroline Murat, Queen of Naples. A few years later in 1868, the Patek Philippe & Co. created a wristwatch for the Countess Kocewicz of Poland. But it wasn't until the 1900's that famous male pilots like Alberto Santos-Dumont and Charles Lindbergh started wearing wristwatches during their flights. Pocket watch sales decreased, and the more reliable, yet inexpensive wristwatch became commonplace. And even today, watches are the number one selling jewelry item in the world!

If you would like to learn some of the more advanced aspects of watch making and watch repair, take a look at some of the classes available at online watch schools. You can usually get started for under $300. Now let's build some watches!

THE PARTS OF A WATCH

Let's take a look at some of the parts that make a watch work. In this section we will be looking at the two most common types of watch movements: a mechanical automatic movement and a quartz movement. The mechanical automatic movement uses stored energy from a mainspring that unwinds and sends power to the gear train, which then moves the hour, minute, and second hands while telling the time. Mechanical movements tend to have more parts than a quartz watch, and are prone to the effects of gravity and temperature, causing the watch to constantly speed up and slow down throughout the day. The mechanical movement requires more maintenance and adjustments, and is more expensive to buy than a quartz movement. Yet, despite these shortcomings, watch enthusiasts easily see that the mechanical watch movement is much more than a timekeeper, it's a work of art, a perfect fusion of form and function. It has a complicated, yet simple design that has been admired for hundreds of years. Note: the *mechanical automatic* watch uses a rotor, which spins freely and winds the mainspring while the watch is being worn. The *mechanical manual* winding watch needs to be wound by hand each day in order for the mainspring to reach its maximum amount of stored energy.

Here are some of the main parts of a mechanical automatic watch that you need to know.

MAINSPRING This spiral spring is the powerhouse of the watch, located in the barrel. It is where the watch's energy is stored. The mainspring is tightly wound around a special type of axle called an arbor, which is rotated during winding and is attached to a large ratchet wheel that is used to prevent the the arbor from rotating backwards and unwinding the mainspring. Then as energy is released, the barrel begins to move, driving the watch gear train. *Note: one end of the spring is attached to the barrel, and one end is attached to the arbor.*

Here is the unwound mainspring.

BARREL This is the cylinder container that houses the mainspring. The barrel is attached to the big **ratchet wheel** on the right. To wind up the mainspring, you have to wind the ratchet wheel. Then as the mainspring unwinds, the stored energy turns the barrel, which turns the gear train.

BALANCE COCK   This is the small bridge that houses the watch regulator (lever, balance wheel, and balance spring).

BALANCE WHEEL   This is the fast moving wheel that oscillates the balance back and forth, and provides a time base to maintain mechanical stability. It oscillates at around 5 beats per second. In the 1960's, the watch company Bulova created an electric watch which involved replacing the balance wheel with a tuning fork. In 1969, Seiko created a quartz watch, which used a quartz crystal (silicon dioxide) in place of the balance wheel. (When a battery sends a charge to a quartz crystal, it vibrates at a constant frequency).

BALANCE   This is the combination of the balance wheel, balance spring, and balance staff.

BALANCE SPRING   This spring controls the half-swing, or "beat" of the balance wheel. Many high quality movements have 18,000 or more beats per hour (9,000 full swings). The higher the BPH, the higher the accuracy of the watch. And when you divide the time into very small increments, like 36,000 BPH or more, you end up with a very precise and stable movement.

Here is the balance cock (the bridge with the + and − symbols), the balance spring, regulator, and balance wheel.

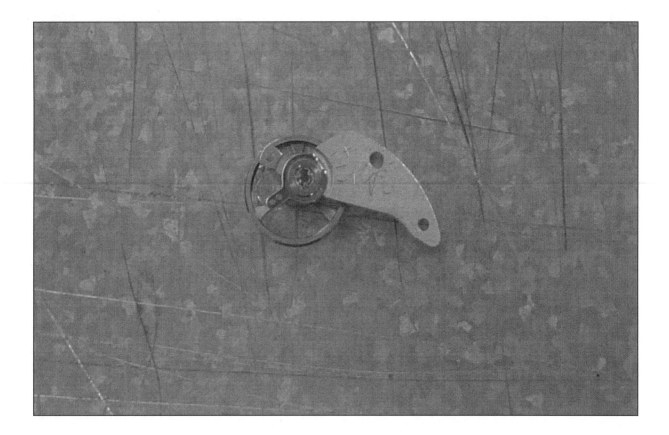

Here is the other side of the balance.

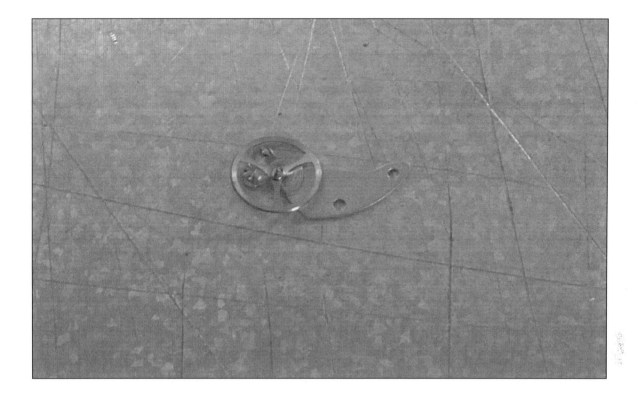

ESCAPEMENT The escapement connects the balance wheel to the escape wheel via the pallet, or "pallet fork". It is the brains of the watch movement. The escapement works by transferring the gear train energy into the oscillating energy of the balance spring. When the escape wheel locks and unlocks (moves), or "escapes", it causes the "ticking" sound that all mechanical watches produce. The escape wheel is not only necessary for maintaining accuracy. It also prevents the mainspring from unwinding completely in a matter of seconds. In other words, the escapement slows down the unwinding process enough to maintain accurate timekeeping.

Below is a diagram of an escape wheel is action. When energy from the gear train moves the pallet fork, it causes the balance wheel to move, which winds and unwinds the balance spring. This causes the "pallet fork" or" pallet lever" to move left and right, which also makes the gear train stop momentarily, regulating the rate at which the mainspring loses energy.

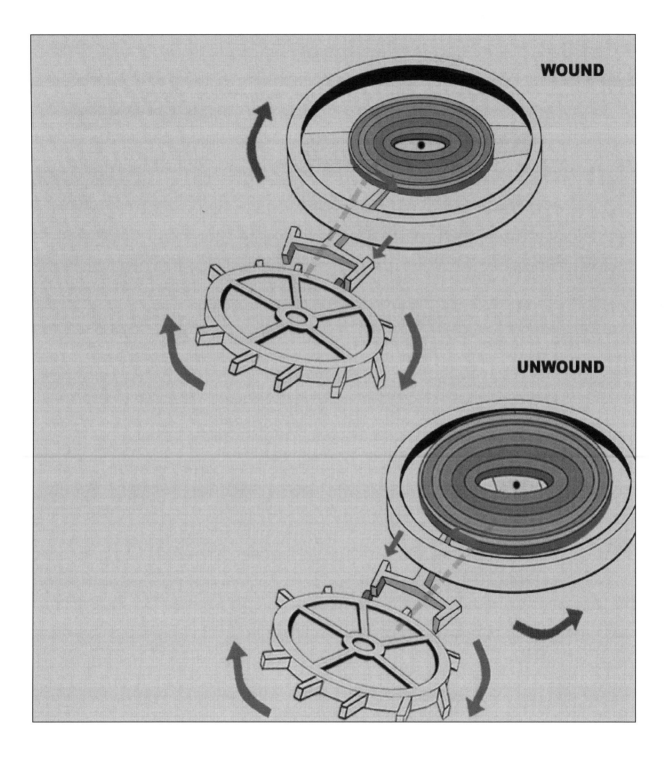

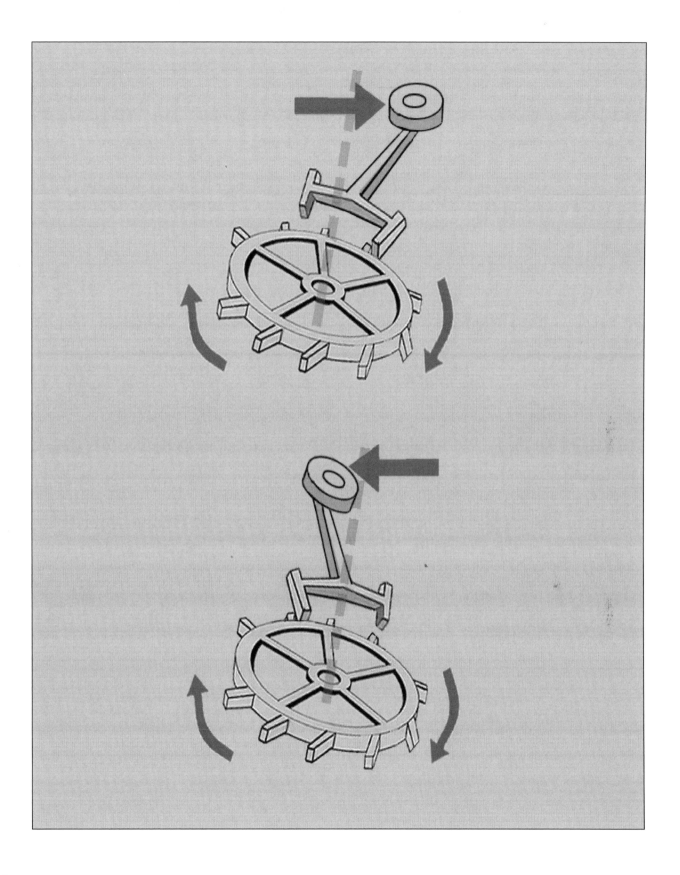

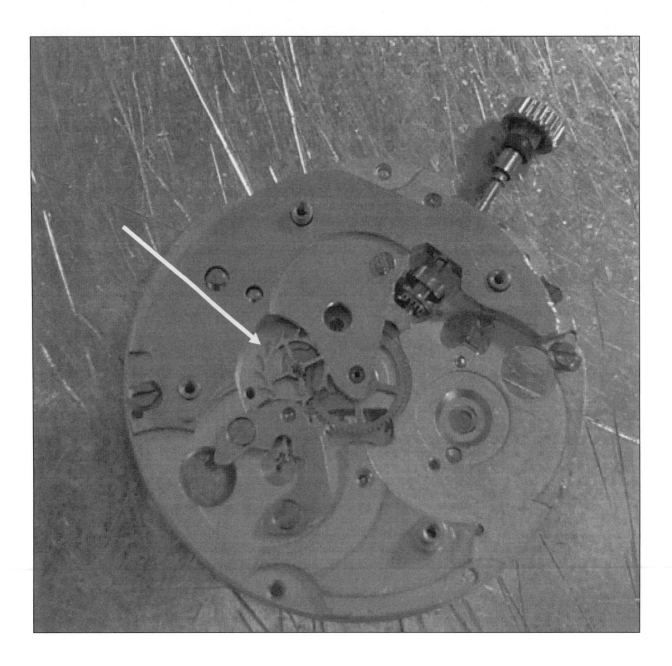

ROTOR This is a weighted semicircle that spins around freely and winds the watch. If there is no rotor on your watch, then you have to wind the watch by hand. Some automatic watches can be wound by the rotor and by hand.

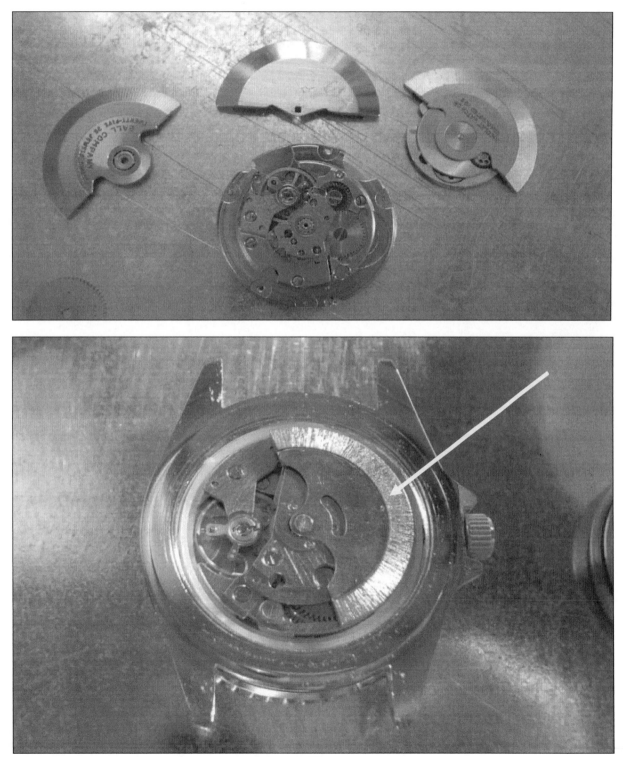

DETENT This is the small button, or pusher that is used to release the stem from the set lever. The movements in most watches cannot be removed from the case unless the stem is removed first. The detent is usually pretty easy to find, but not always. Sometimes you have to push the crown in, or pull it out to view the detent. The detent is also referred to as the *set lever pushpin*.

SET LEVER SCREW If your watch movement has a small screw instead of a detent, it is called a spring loaded set lever screw, or setting lever screw. To remove the stem, rotate the screw counter clockwise a ¼ turn at a time, then try to pull out the stem by gently pushing it in and out. If it doesn't come out, then rotate another ¼ turn and try again. Keep doing this until the crown is able to be pulled out. **Warning: if you loosen this screw too much, the setting mechanism will become disassembled. Only loosen the set lever enough so that the stem can be pulled out.**

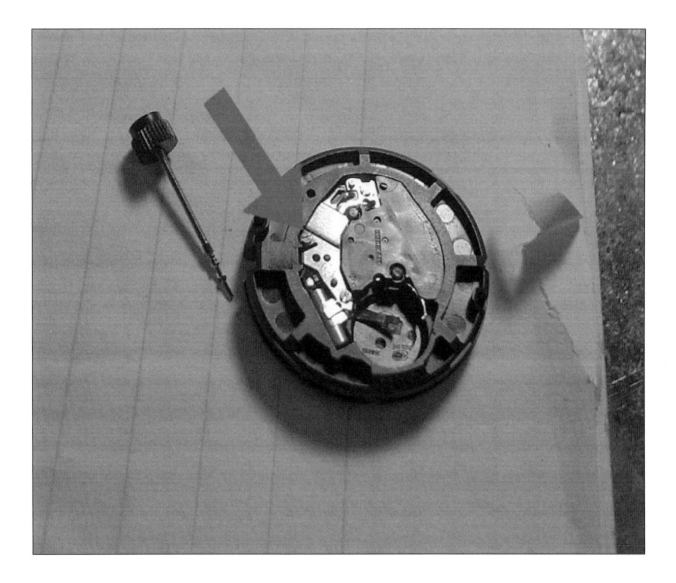

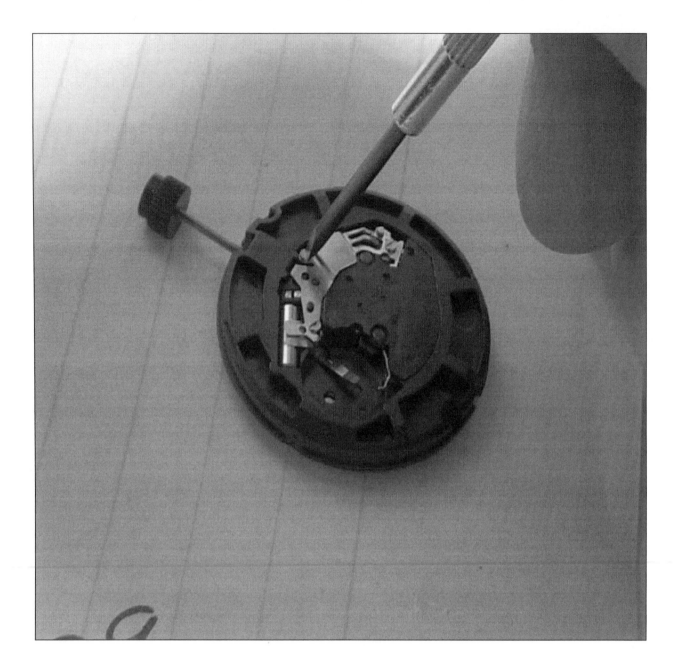

DIAL The dial is the face of the watch. It displays the hour, minute, and second numerals, which are also known as indicators, or indices. The dial on the bottom of this page is one of my favorites from www.ofrei.com. It cost only $5. I've made plenty of watches with this dial. It's simple and to the point, and it looks good.

If you are interested in making a one of a kind watch, get a dial from www.10watches.com. The 28.5 mm dial below has superluminova painted indices and cost around $30.

Here are some more unbranded 28.5 mm watch dials from Noah Fuller at www.10watches.com. They start at around $15. If you are going to be building watches with Seiko parts, then this is one site you will need to visit.

Here is some more of Noah Fuller's Seiko watches. He sells these watches, and also the individual parts.

CROWN   The watch's winding knob that screws into the stem and also allows you to set the day, date, and the time. When the crown is pushed in, the watch is ready to wear. When the crown is pulled out, the time can be set. On some watches, you will have to pull out the crown again to the next position in order to adjust the date. On other watches, you will have to pull out the crown and turn it counter clockwise to adjust the date, and clockwise to adjust the day. It's always a good idea to have extra crowns handy when working on different types of watches. You can buy an assorted crown kit online at www.esslinger.com for around $35.

CROWN TUBE If you have a waterproof watch with a screw down crown, then you have a crown tube in your watch case. This is the small threaded barrel that the crown screws into. This tube screws right into the watch case, and can be unscrewed with needle nose pliers. Be careful not to damage the threads if changing the crown tube.

STEM The stem is the thin, winding shaft that connects the crown to the movement. In most watches, the stem must be removed before the movement can come out. The stem is divided into several sections called the *post* (which screws into the crown), *set lever*, *clutch key*, and *positioner*. The small gap between the clutch key and post is where the set lever makes contact with the stem, and holds it in place. Pushing on the detent, or unscrewing the set lever screw, will release this pressure, and allow the stem to come out of the movement.

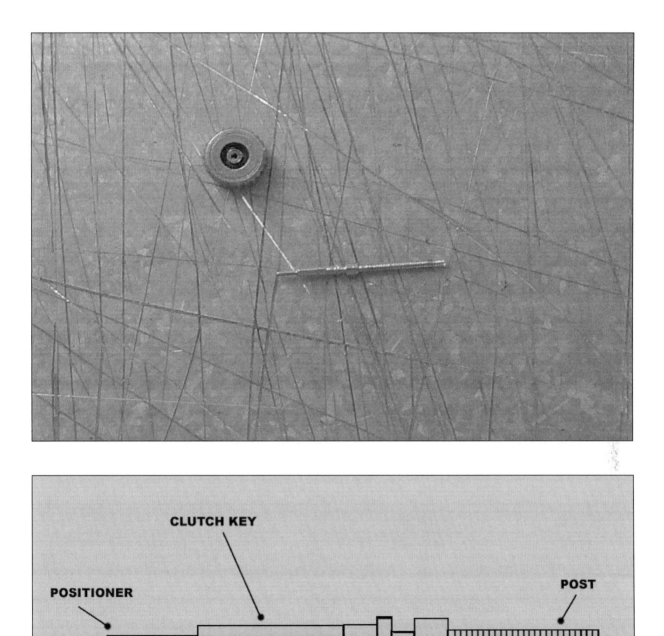

Let's take a look at how the stem works on a typical watch. When the stem is pulled out, the setting lever moves backward, engaging the clutch lever (yoke). The clutch lever then causes the intermediate wheel and clutch (sliding pinion) to connect together, while the winding pinion disengages. At this point, any rotation of the stem will move the intermediate wheel, which touches the minute wheel and hour wheel. You can now set the time. If you push the stem back in, then the opposite happens, and the clutch engages the winding pinion, allowing you to wind up the mainspring. If your watch is not made to be wound by hand, then it does not have a winding pinion. *Note: if you push the set lever detent, or unscrew the set lever screw a few turns, the stem will disengage from the set lever, and can then be pulled out of the movement.* Check out the parts below.

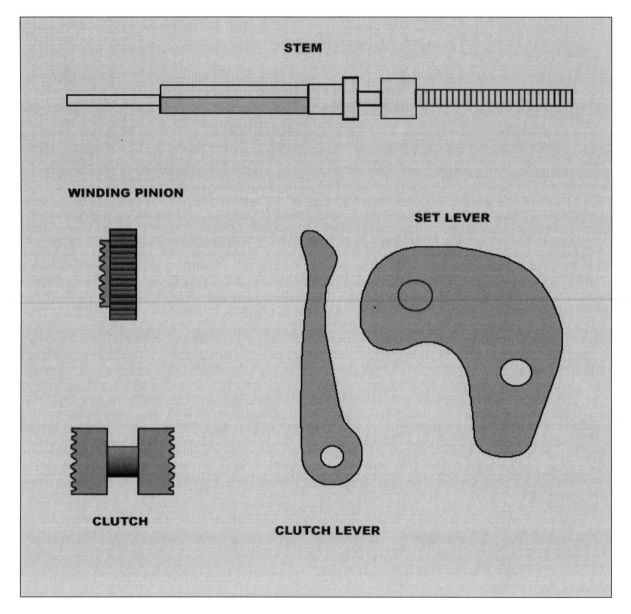

STEM

WINDING PINION

SET LEVER

CLUTCH

CLUTCH LEVER

When the stem is pushed in, the clutch comes in contact with the winding pinion. When the stem is pulled out, the clutch touches the intermediate wheel, allowing you to set the time.

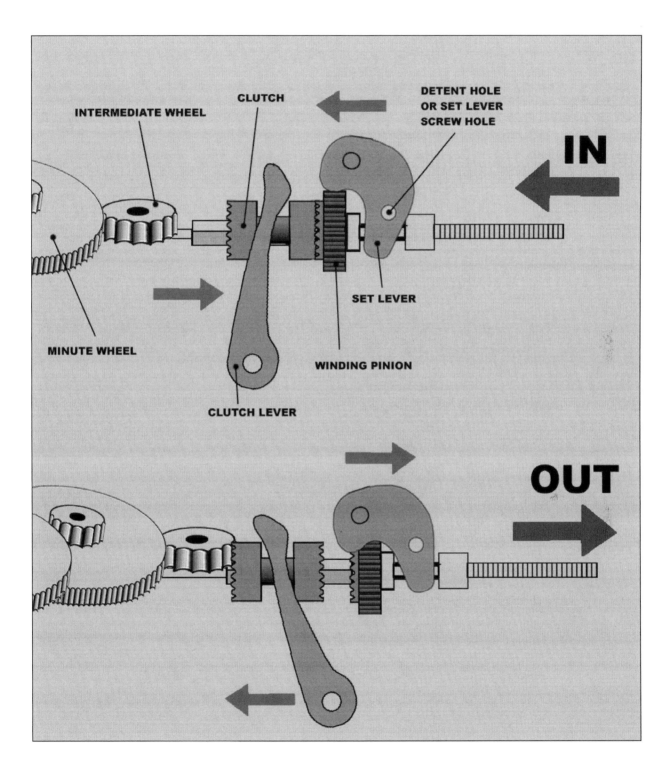

Notice the clutch and intermediate wheel in the picture below.

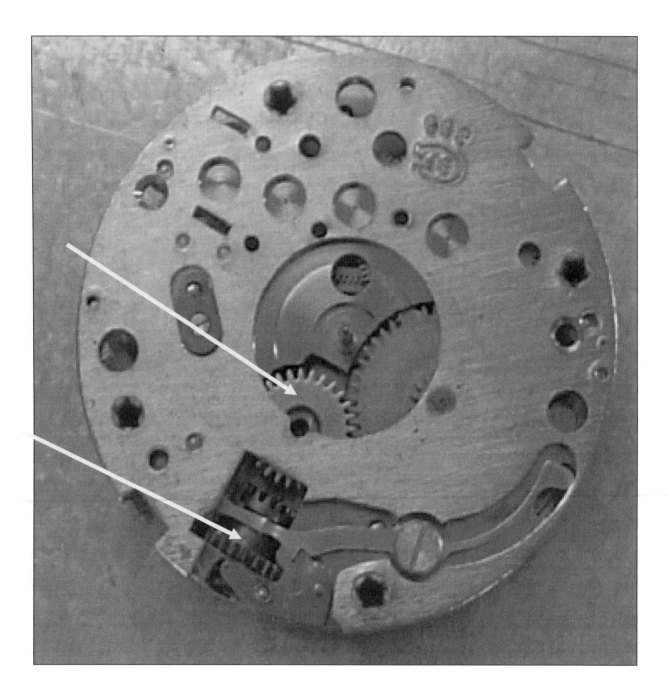

DIAL HANDS   Watch hands are the parts that point to the watch's hour, minute, and second numerals, or indices. If you know the diameter of the hour, minute, and second hand shaft (fourth wheel pinion, cannon pinion, and hour wheel), then you know what size hands you need to buy for your watch. Hands are measured in millimeters. Some common sizes for quartz watch hands are 1.20mm for the hour hand, .70mm for the minute hand, and .20mm for the second hand. Some common sizes for diving watch hands with automatic movements are 1.50mm for the hour hand, .90mm for the minute hand, and .25mm for the second hand. *Note: the hands below are from www.ofrei.com.*

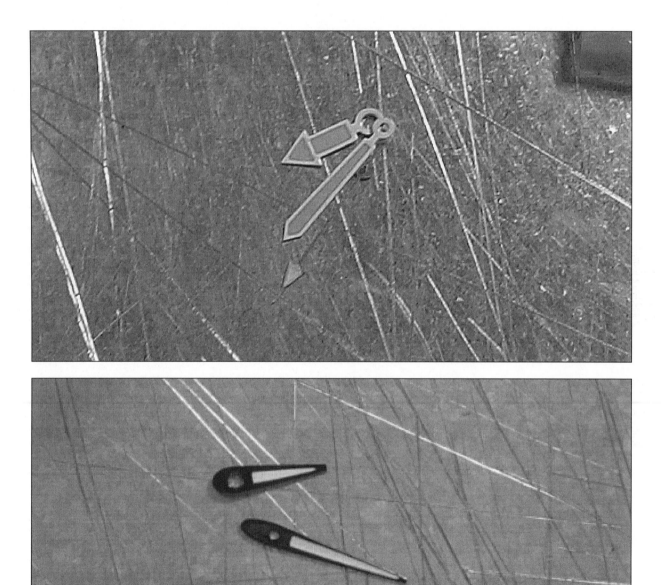

A nice set of watch hands can bring your watch to life. You can find some very cool watch hands on Ebay for the Seiko 7s26 movement. The sizes for these hands are 150/90/25.

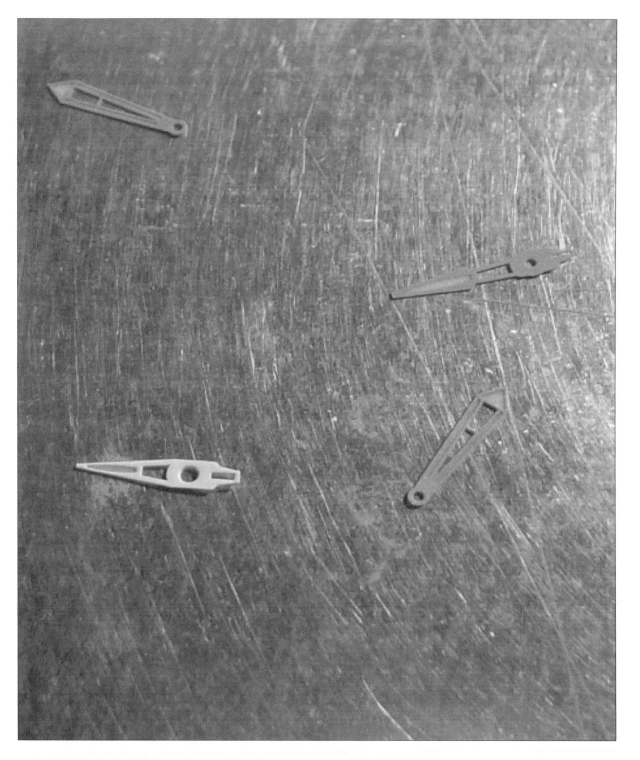

Another great source for Seiko watch hands is a seller by the name of *Yobokies* from Hong Kong, *Seiko Boy* spelled backwards. Who doesn't love a good Seiko? His website address is:

http://s161.photobucket.com/home/yobokies/index

Here is some more of *Yobokies* work.

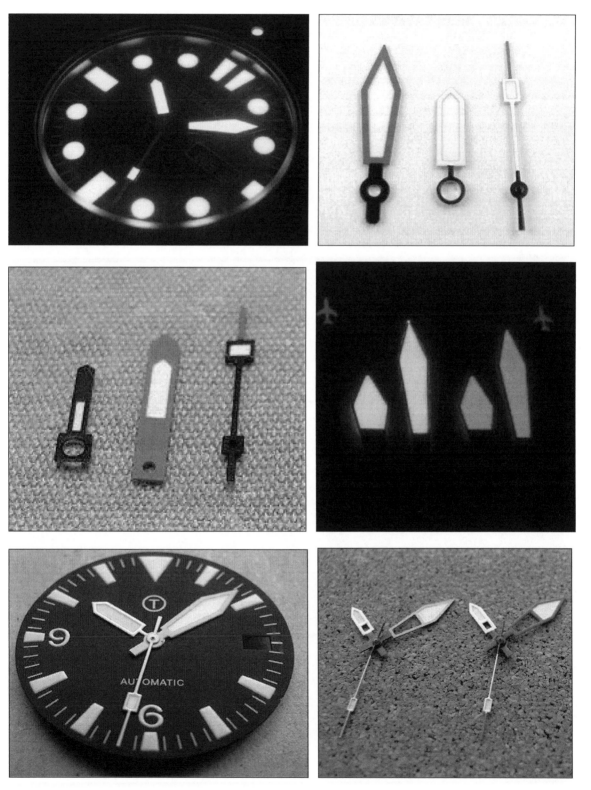

The hands on a Luminox watch contain small radioactive tubes filled with Tritium. These tubes remain lit up for 25 years or more. The words "T-SWISS" on the dial let you know that the watch emits a low level of radiation from the Tritium tubes.

Here is a close-up of the watch hands and where they are located on a movement.

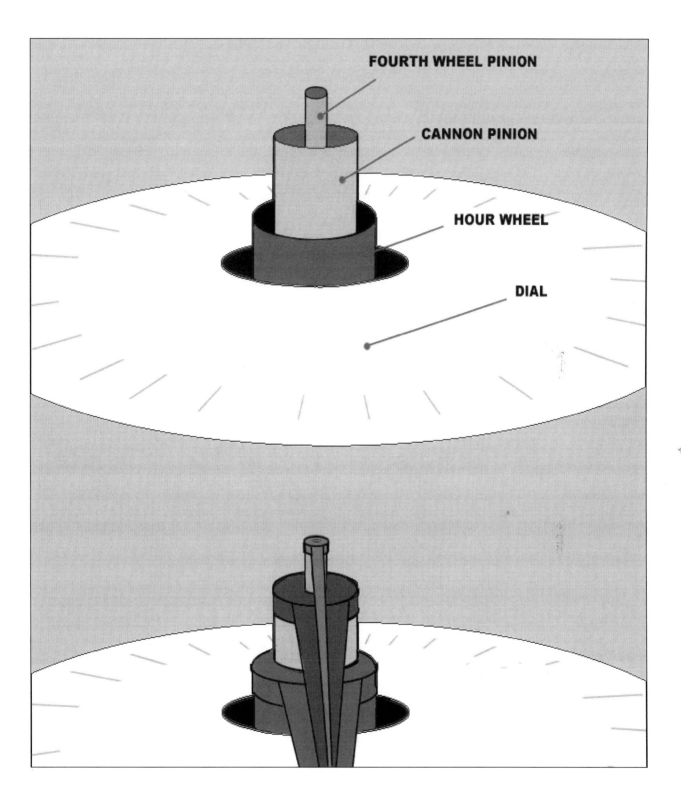

Here is another view of the gears which turn the watch hands. *Note: the fourth wheel pinion is also called the seconds pinion because it turns the second hand.*

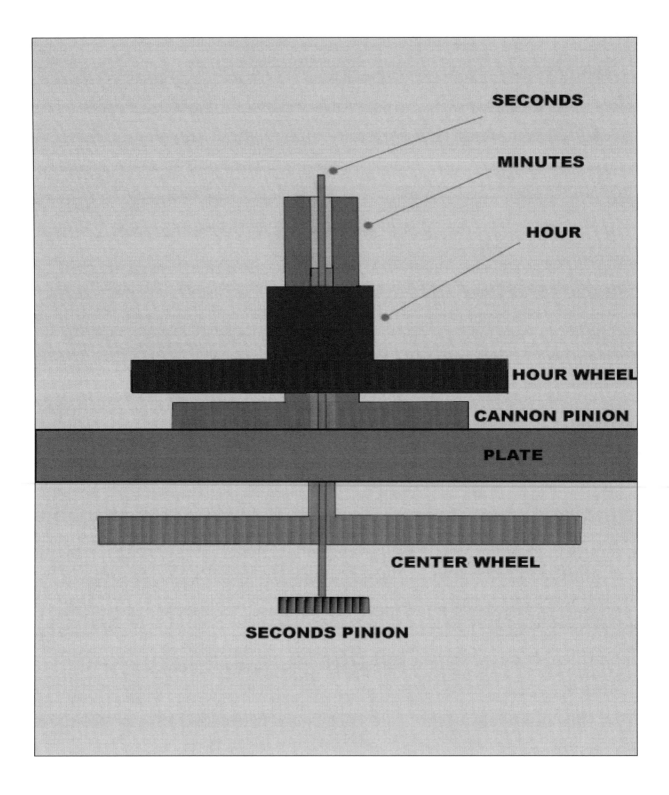

SECONDS

MINUTES

HOUR

HOUR WHEEL

CANNON PINION

PLATE

CENTER WHEEL

SECONDS PINION

MOVEMENT
This is the engine of the watch, composed of the internal parts which make it tick. Most movements nowadays are mechanical or quartz, or a combination of the two, called kinetic movements, which use a rotor, capacitor, and quartz crystal. Other types of watch movements exist, like solar powered movements, and heat powered movements. And don't forget about digital movements.

MECHANICAL MOVEMENT
This is a watch movement that uses a mainspring as its main power source. Mechanical watch movements have an accuracy of + or - 10 minutes per month, or less. Below is a picture of a self winding, automatic mechanical movement in its case.

Here is a manual wind, mechanical movement. The mainspring needs to be wound by hand every day in order to keep it running. There is no rotor on this watch movement.

What are some common movements found in quartz and automatic watches?

ETA SA – This swiss company is formed by the merger of ETA and Ebauches SA (ESA). It is part of the *Swatch Group* (Swatch, ETA, Valjoux, Piguet, Omega, Longines, Hamilton, Blancpain, Breguet, Tiffany & Co., and many more). ETA dominates the production of high end movements, and can be found in a countless number of popular watches like Breitling, Fortis, Cartier, IWC, Oris, Eterna, Tissot and Tag Heuer. The main thing to remember about ETA is accuracy. Their movements are known to be very precise, in part due to their superior mainspring. You can find ETA 2824 and 2892 movements for around $130 - $250 on Ebay. Keep in mind certain watches like the Rolex Tudor Submariner come with a top grade ETA 2824 movement and cost several thousand dollars in retail stores. The 2824 has a BPH (beats per hour) of 28,800 and a power reserve of around 40 hours.

ETA also manufactures many popular quartz movements under the ETA or ESA name. The ETA 805.114 is one of my favorites. It keeps great time and only cost around $10.

Valjoux - This swiss company is also owned by ETA. The Valjoux 7750 is one of the best chronograph movements on the market. It is also a 28,800 BPH movement with a power reserve of 42 hours. It can be found in watches that cost over $6000. This movement cost around $450 at www.ofrei.com.

Unitas – These movements are also made by ETA. If you are looking for a big pilot watch or pocket watch, then the (16.5 Ligne, 36.6mm) Unitas 6497 might be what you're looking for. You can find them for around $130 online.

Seiko Watch Corp. – Seiko, which is a subsidiary of the *Seiko Holdings Corp.* out of Japan, makes great mechanical and quartz movements in house at affordable prices. They also offer some of the world's most expensive watches in their Credor line ($500,000 for a Credor Juri which offers a BPH of over 43,000). One of the more common Seiko automatic workhorses, the 7S26, is well known for its amazing durability and indestructible rotor. They say this movement can last forever. It puts out 21,800 BPH and has 21 jewels. Some say it is even possible to get this movement in the +/- 2 seconds a day range. Not bad for a watch movement that only cost around $45 at www.10watches.com.

As far as quartz movements go, Seiko doesn't just make them, they invented them back in 1969, changing the watch industry forever. Quartz moevemnts are extremely accurate, with some boasting an accuracy of +/- 10 seconds a year (Seiko Astron). You can find a bunch of Seiko quartz movements online at www.ofrei.com.

Miyota – Miyota is a Japanese company owned by the *Citizen Watch Co., LTD*. Citizen is one of the largest watch manufacturers in the world, so if you buy a used watch lot on Ebay, chances are you will come across a Miyota movement or two. One of Miyota's popular automatic movements is the 8215. It competes with the ETA 2824 in reliability and durability, but at a much lower cost (around $40 at www.ofrei.com). It has a BPH of 21,600 with 21 jewels. You can find this movement in Citizen, Invicta, and Festina watches.

The quartz Miyota movements can be found in Citizen, Bulova, Miyota, Adee Kaye, and Wittnauer watches. My favorite is the Miyota 2115, which cost around $10. It's cheap, yet very accurate. You can find these movements at www.ofrei.com, www.esslinger.com, and www.jewelerssupplies.com.

Harley Ronda – This swiss company makes high quality quartz watch movements for Tag Heuer, Traser, Luminox, Doxa, Orsa, and many more. The Ronda 715 is a popular movement found in many good watches.

ISA Swiss - You can find quality ISA movements in Croton, Android, Invicta, and Oniss watches.

43

Here is a *Durowe 7425* hand winding movement that I got on Ebay for a few bucks.

QUARTZ MOVEMENT This is a watch movement that uses a battery, quartz crystal, and stepping motor as its main power source. Quartz oscillates at 32,768 Hz. These watches are very accurate, and can gain or lose around 10 seconds per month or less.

KINETIC MOVEMENT This type of watch movement combines the accuracy of a quartz watch with the self-winding abilities of some mechanical watches. It has both a rotor and an energy storage device similar to a battery, which is called a *kinetic energy storage unit (ESU),* or sometimes referred to as a capacitor. Once fully charged (over 20,000 rotor swings), the watch can run for a long time, usually 1-6 months. If you really hate winding your watch, then the auto relay kinetic watches might be up your alley. They claim a 4 year run time when fully charged. Below is a picture of a kinetic movement. The ESU looks very similar to a standard watch battery. When buying older kinetic watches keep in mind that the ESU can go bad over time, especially if allowed to discharge completely. A bad ESU means your watch won't be able to store much energy. When replacing the ESU and its insulation, unscrew the rotor and rotor wheel. Then unscrew two more small screws and replace the ESU with a new one.

Below is a quick summary of the project. All of the screws involved should be magnetized, but be careful, they are very small and can get lost easily. Pay special attention to the positioning of the red insulation.

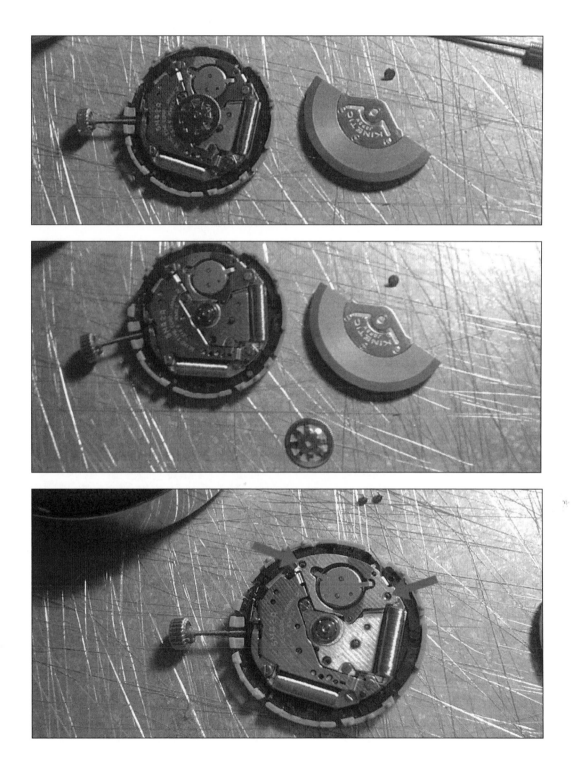

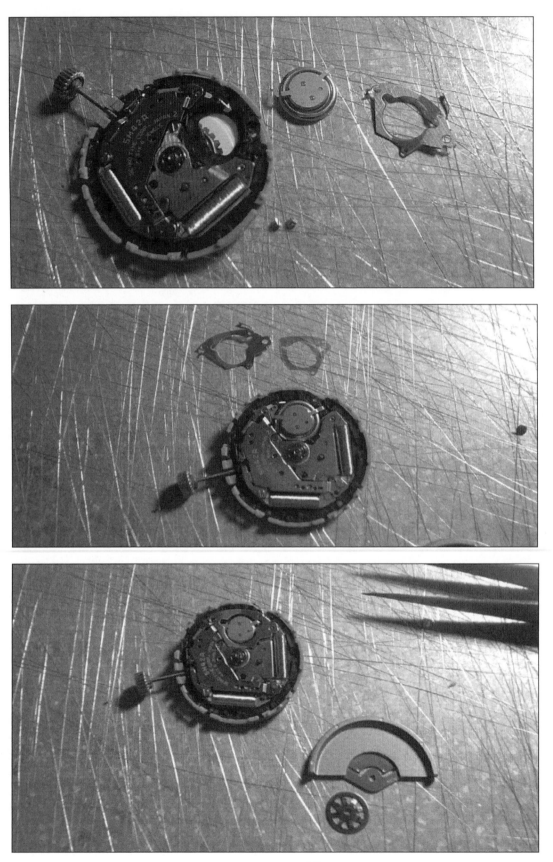

SKELETON WATCH MOVEMENT The skeleton movement was created for the watch aficionado who wants to view the inner workings of the watch. To do this, the plates and bridges need to have sections cut out, allowing you to see the working movement. Here is an attractive Chinese made 2650G hand winding mechanical movement from www.ofrei.com. It retails for only $10.50.

CASE   The case is the protective covering that protects the watch movement.

CASE BACK   This is the metal cap on the back of the watch case. It is usually removed in order to work on the watch movement. Most case backs can be unscrewed with a special tool, or pried off with a pocket knife.

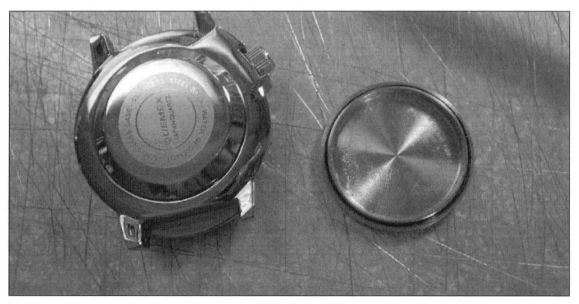

MOVEMENT HOLDER   Movement holders are plastic casing rings that hold the watch movement securely inside the watch case. They are the foundation of most watch projects. If you can't hold a movement in place, then you can't adequately build a watch. These holders come in sizes ranging from 3 3/4 Lignes all the way up to 11 ½ Lignes. (1 Ligne is equal to 2.256mm). Movement holders can also be fabricated out of tubes of pliable putty like Speedi-Fit. I like to have plenty of plastic movement holders in stock so I can switch out movements with ease. You can buy movement holder kits at www.ofrei.com.

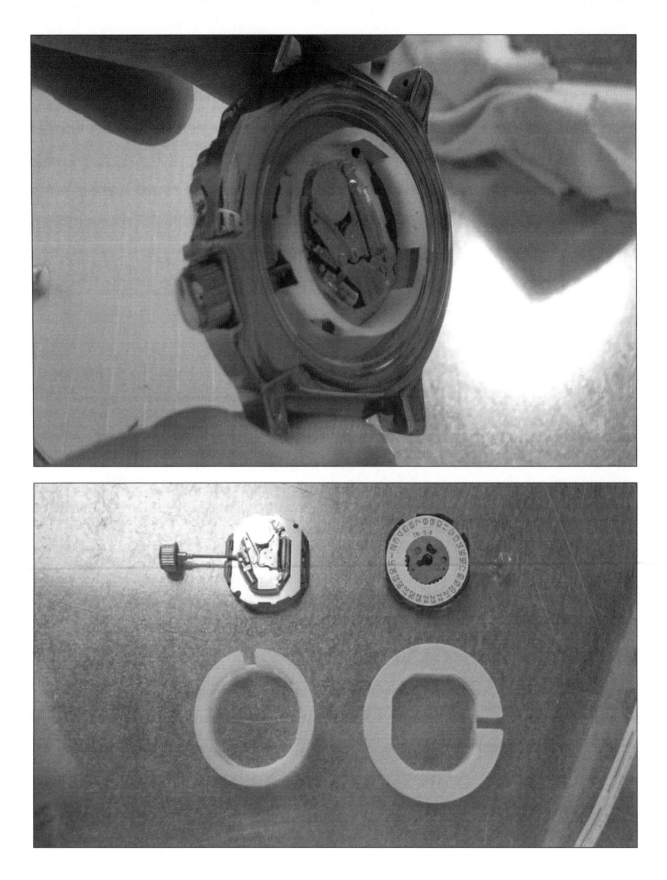

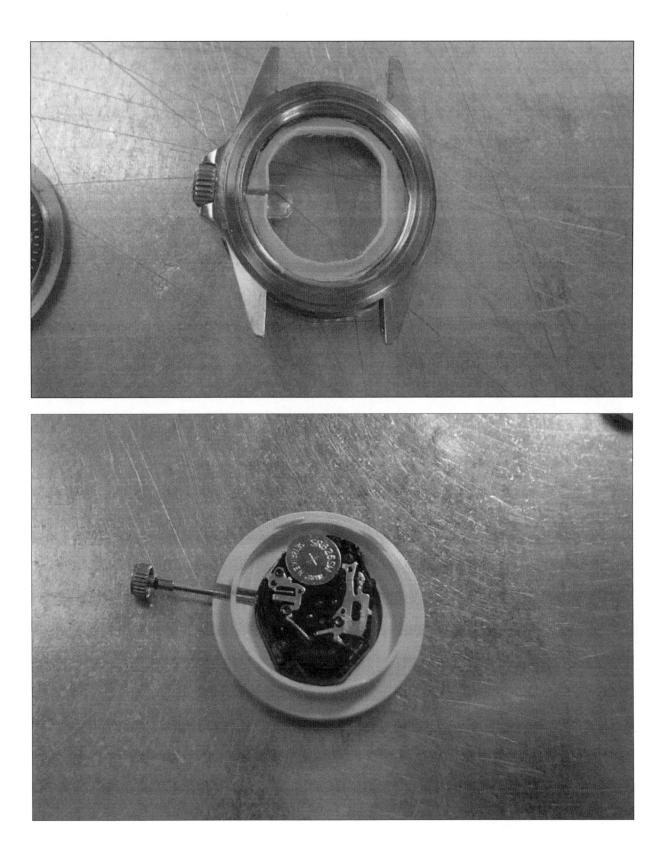

Here is a 6 ¾ Ligne movement and holder.

Here is an ETA 805.114 (11 ½ Ligne) movement and holder.

Here is a mechanical 11 ½ Ligne movement with holder.

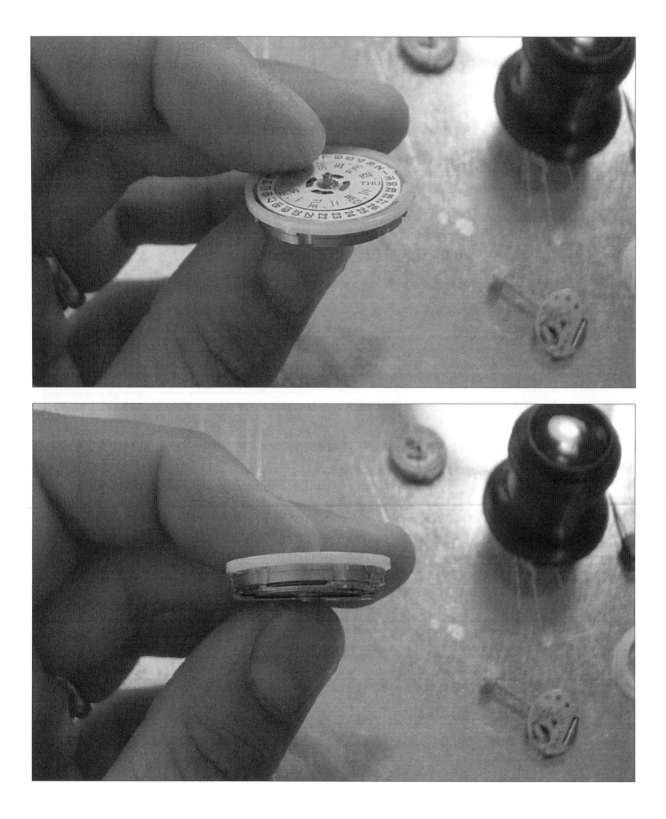

Here is another mechanical watch movement and holder that fits snugly inside its case.

Below is a chart showing some of the most common movement shapes and sizes measured in Lignes. If you order an 11 ½ Ligne movement, like a quartz ETA 805.114, then it will have a diameter of 26.5 mm. Note: there are other shapes and sizes of movements available, like the Miyota 2117. It is a round 10 ½ Ligne movement mounted on a square chip.

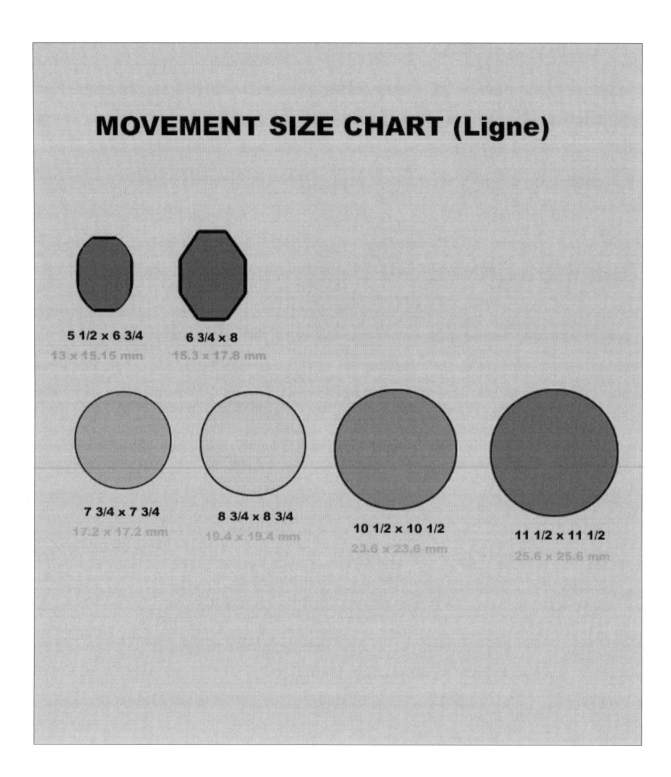

MOVEMENT SIZE CHART (Ligne)

5 1/2 x 6 3/4
13 x 15.15 mm

6 3/4 x 8
15.3 x 17.8 mm

7 3/4 x 7 3/4
17.2 x 17.2 mm

8 3/4 x 8 3/4
19.4 x 19.4 mm

10 1/2 x 10 1/2
23.6 x 23.6 mm

11 1/2 x 11 1/2
25.6 x 25.6 mm

Here is a Miyota 2117 movement and a 10 ½ Ligne movement holder.

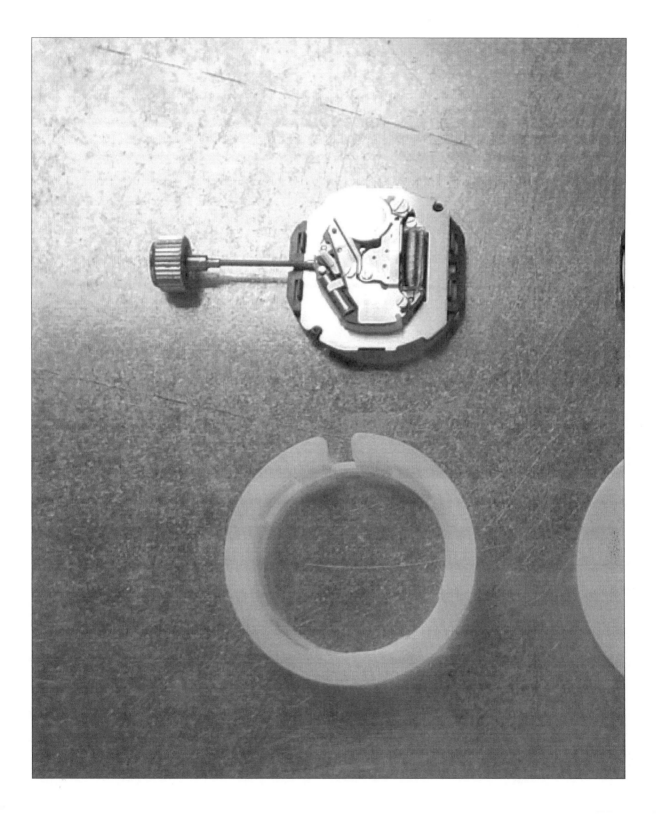

You can take a larger movement holder and change its size if needed. The movement holder on the right had to be filed down to fit inside the watch case and hold the movement securely in place. The movement holder needs to prevent the watch movement from changing position, especially when you are pulling out and pushing in the crown.

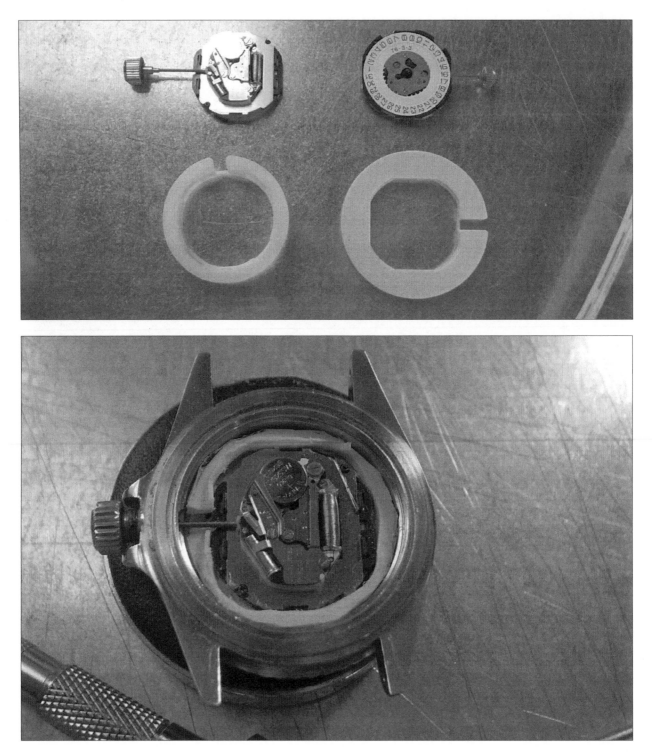

Below is a 5 ½ Ligne movement holder, case, and dial.

Here is a 6 ¾ Ligne movement holder, movement, stem, crown, and case. The holder had to be filed down a bit in order for the case to screw on.

The movement holder can be filed down around the edges, too, if needed.

CRYSTAL This is the window that protects the watch dial. It is usually made out of plastic (acrylic), mineral glass, or sapphire, with sapphire being the most expensive.

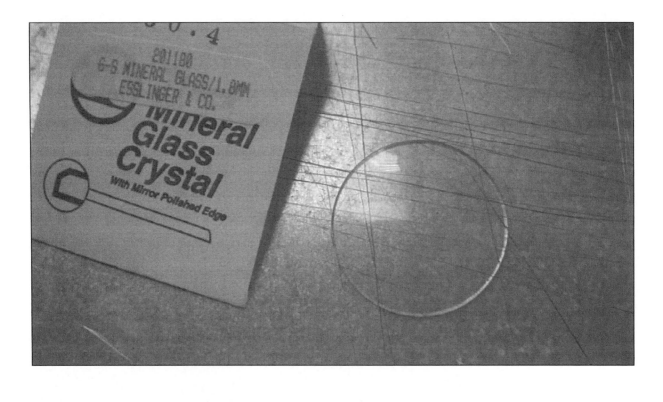

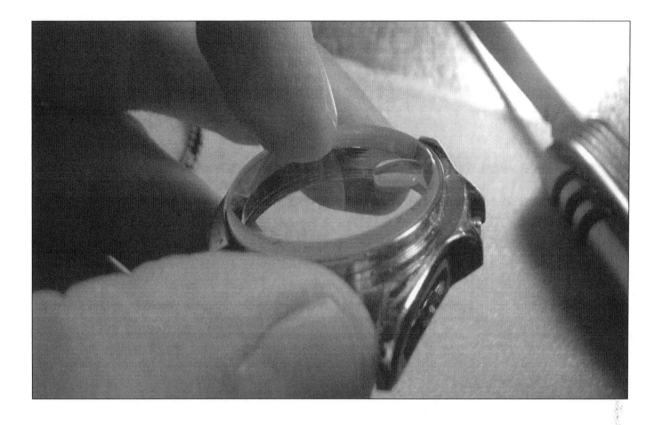

SPRING BARS These spring loaded barrels use compressed energy to connect the watch band to the watch lugs.

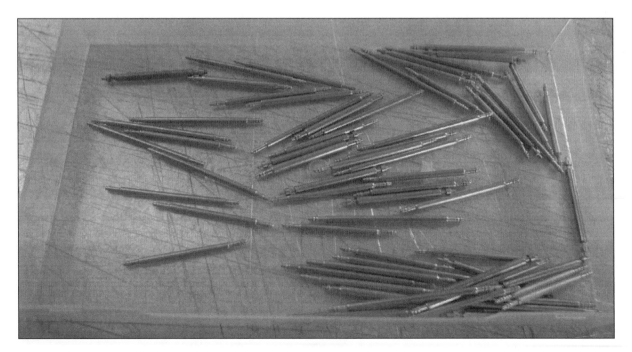

Have a bunch of spring bars and need to organize them? If you fully compress a spring bar with your caliper, you can get a good indication of the spring bar size. The spring bar pictured below is 18mm.

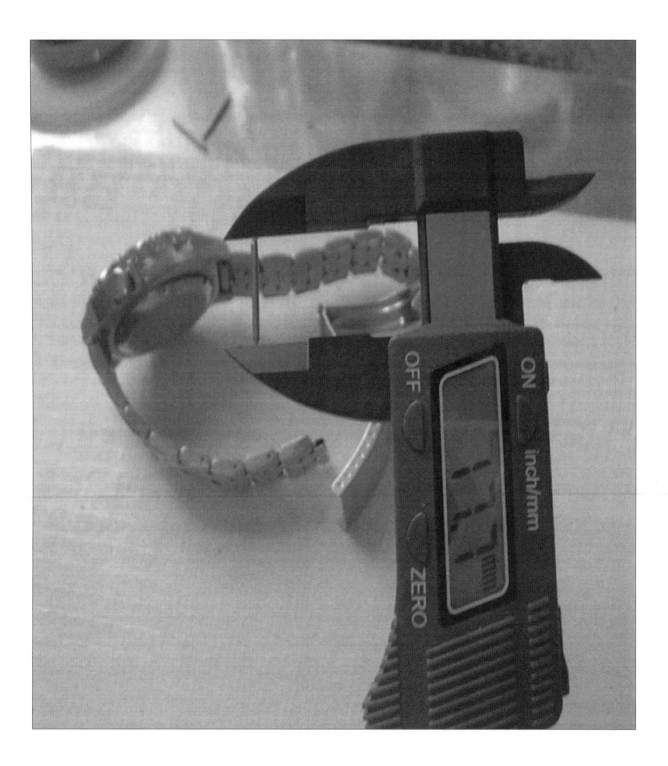

Here is a diagram showing the spring bar and link pins on a watch bracelet.

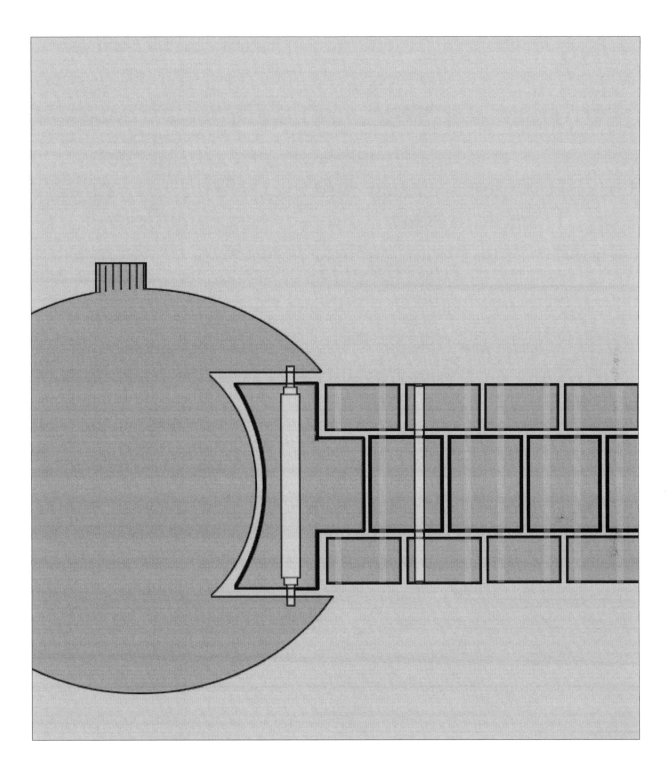

BAND A bracelet is a metal watch band. A soft band, made from leather, rubber, or plastic is usually referred to as a watch strap, or just "band".

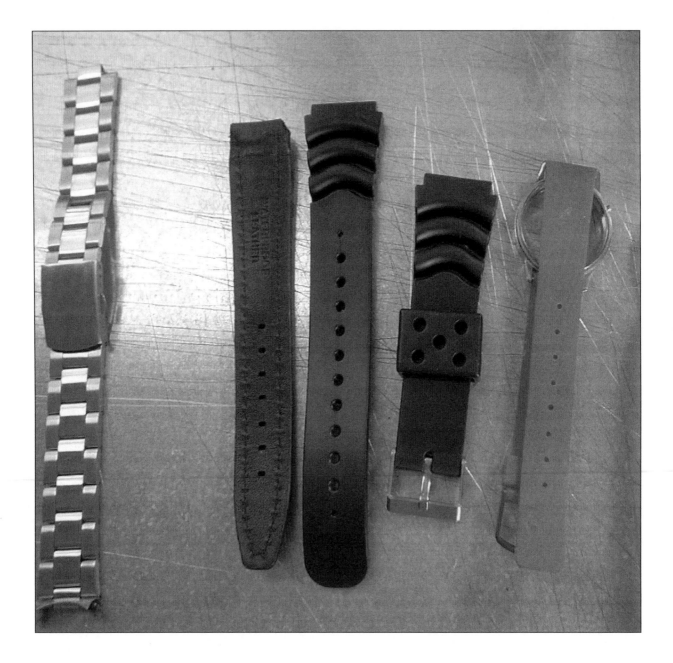

Here is the same watch with two different bands. The first is a stainless steel bracelet and the second is a rubber strap with green stitching. Flexible metal bracelets, like the one pictured below, are made by the companies *Spiedel* and *Flex-On*.

The shark mesh bracelet shown below is not only comfortable, but super strong. The mesh bands are my favorite type of diving band. These are available at www.strapcode.com for $63.

Below is a generic rubber diving band. The folds in the band allow you to put the watch on extra tight over your wet suit without adding too much tension to the spring bars. In very deep saturation dives, the wet suit will shrink, causing the band to loosen up, which is why you need the band (not the spring bars) to handle additional tension above the water. Diving watches by definition can handle dives of 100 meters (330 ft.) or more without malfunctioning. The first diving watch on record is the Omega Marine from 1932. Shortly thereafter, Blancpain, Rolex, and Doxa began producing innovative diving watches.

BEZEL The watch bezel is the rotating ring, bezel spring, and bezel insert that borders the watch crystal. Normally, bezels are used to measure time, speed, or distance. But, they can measure other functions, too, like diving decompression stops. Unidirectional Bezels that spin in one direction are used on most diving watches. Bi-directional bezels are used for mathematical calculations, like measuring speed (tachymeter, or tachometer).

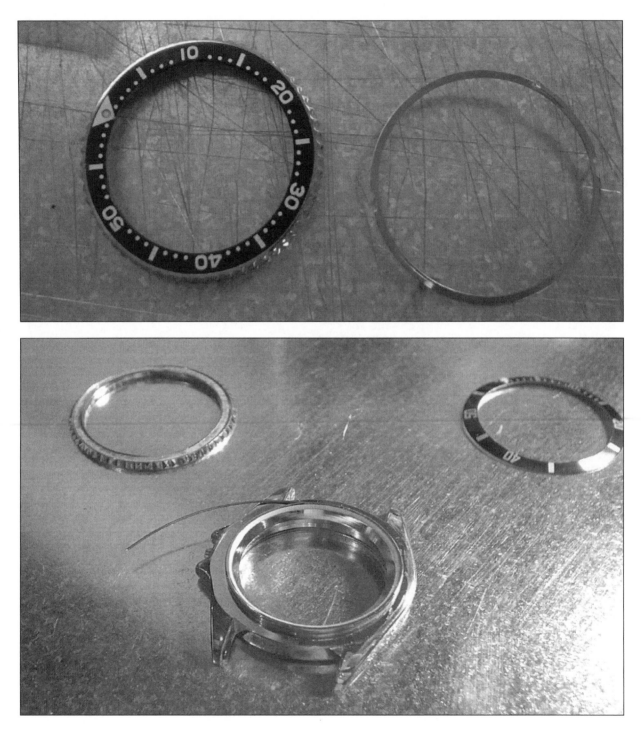

REGULATOR   The regulator is a small lever positioned above the balance wheel that speeds up or slows down a mechanical watch movement. If you move the lever towards the "F" (fast) indicator, the movement will run faster. If you move the lever in the opposite direction towards the "S" (slow or retard) indicator, the movement will run slower.

GASKET A gasket is a thin rubber ring placed in between the watch case and case back to prevent water from flowing into the case. Smaller gaskets can also be used on waterproof watch crowns. A lubricant like silicone is used on the gasket to help maintain water resistance. You can buy an assorted gasket kit from esslinger.com or ofrei.com for around $10. It's always a good idea to put a new gasket on an old or used watch that you just bought. So make sure you have several sizes in stock.

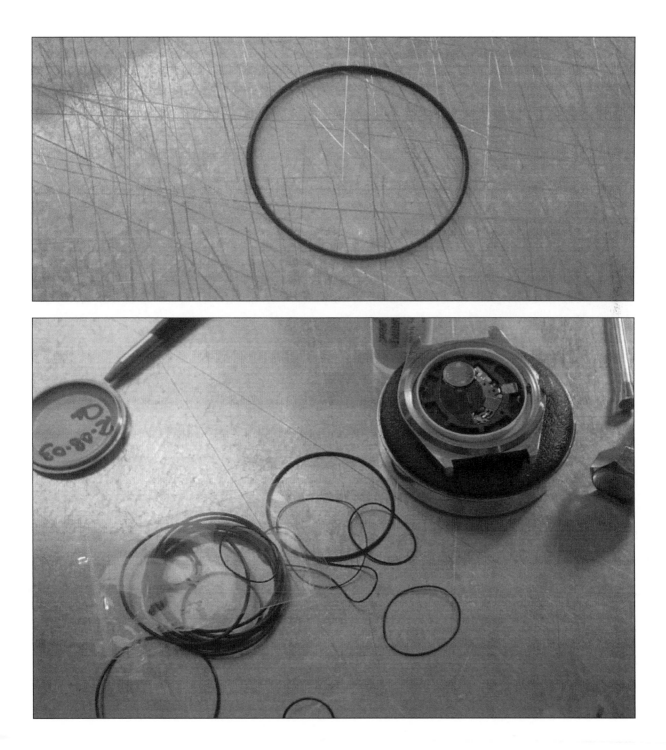

FRICTION GASKET This is the small plastic ring that holds diving watch crystals in place. A case press or crystal press is used to push the crystal in position. If your watch does not have a friction gasket, then it probably uses glue, like Hypo Cement, to hold the crystal in place.

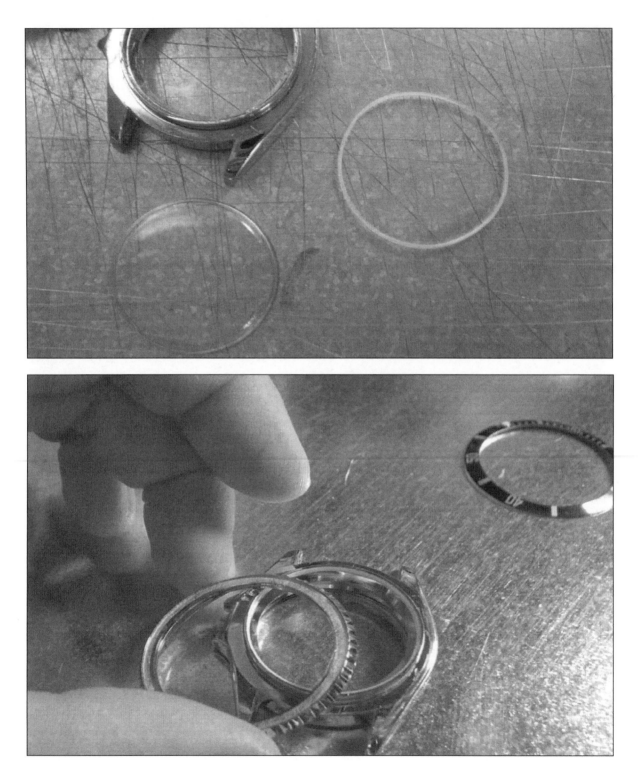

CHAPTER RING A chapter ring is a second indicator that is separate from the watch dial. These are popular on Seiko diving watches. Often, the crystal will need to be removed in order to replace the chapter ring. On other watches, you can get to the chapter ring by simply opening up the case back.

Here is the chapter ring with the dial and hands.

LUGS These are the extended parts of the case that the spring bars are attached to.

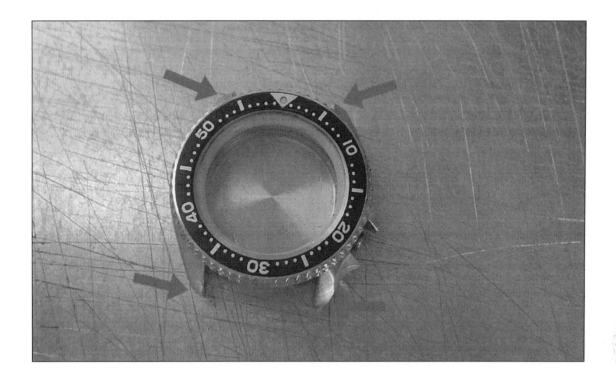

JEWELS These are synthetic rubies or sapphires, used to reduce friction in places where ball bearings are too large to use. The balance of any decent mechanical watch will always be jewelled, since that is where much of the watch's wear and tear occurs at.

PUSHERS These are small buttons protruding from the watch case, usually used for stopwatch or timing functions.

PLATES Two plates on a mechanical watch movement form a frame that houses all of the springs, gears, wheels, pinions, screws, and bridges. There are two sides to a watch movement, the bottom plate and the top plate.

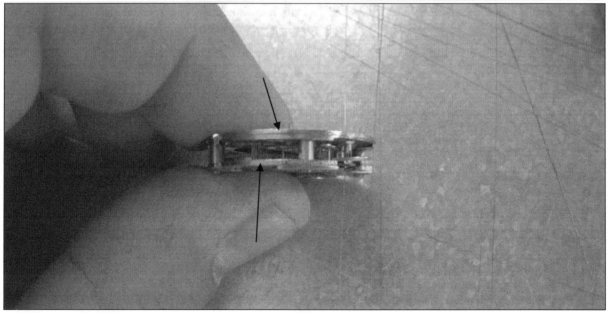

Here are the same two plates.

BRIDGE A smaller plate that is screwed into one of the two bigger plates.

GEAR TRAIN   The gear train is all of the small gears, or wheels, which take power from the balance spring and pallet, and send it to the watch hands.   The gear train consists of the **center wheel** (one revolution per hour, drives the minute hand, and gets power from the mainspring barrel), **third wheel** (two revolutions per hour, and gets power from the center wheel), **fourth wheel** (one revolution per minute, drives the second hand, and gets power from the third wheel), and **escape wheel** (over 1000 revolutions per hour, and gets power from the fourth wheel).   The mainspring barrel is considered the first wheel, and the center wheel is considered the second wheel.   The power for the gear train starts at the mainspring, located in the barrel, and then makes its way to the balance wheel.   **Note: many of the wheels in the gear train have pinions, or small gears, which are not shown in the diagram on the next page.**

Let's look at a diagram of the watch's power train.   Stored energy (from winding the watch) comes from the mainspring, which is located inside the barrel, and is sent through the gears (which turn the hands), and then to the balance spring (which controls the speed of the gear train and watch).   *Note: in order to keep the diagram simplified, the small pinion gears, which are located above or below certain wheels, are not shown in this diagram.   They are used to connect some of wheels together.*

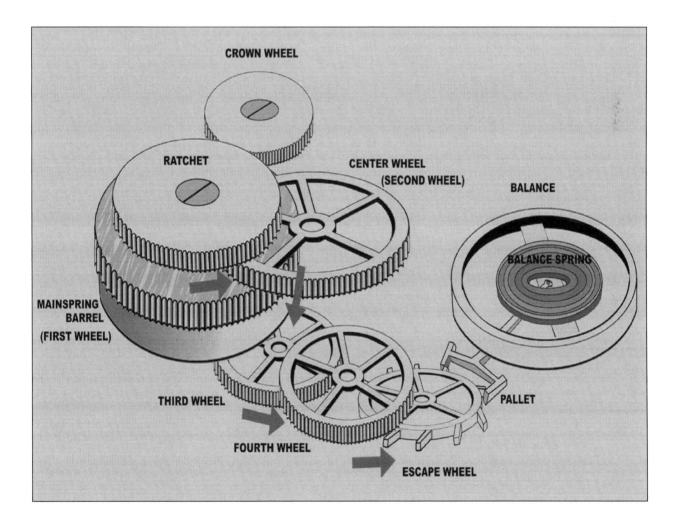

Here is an example of how a pinion is connected to the larger hour wheel.

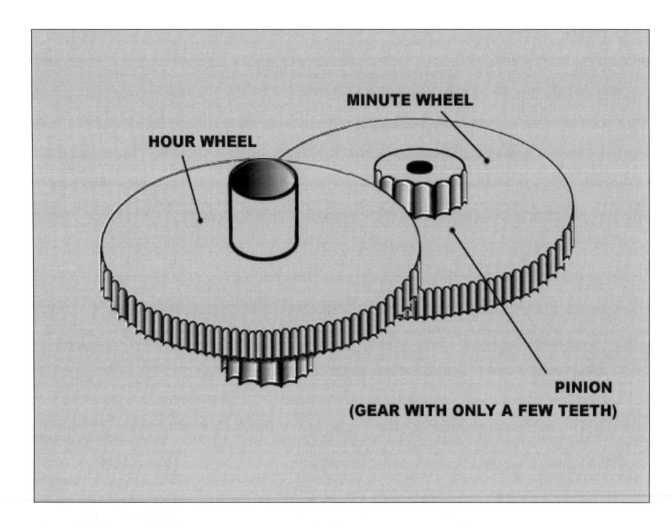

Next we are going to look at the balance and regulator on a mechanical watch. The regulator, or regulator lever, allows you to adjust the tension in the balance spring, which makes its coil oscillate faster or slower. The balance spring speed will affect how quickly the mainspring winds down, and that is how the speed of the watch is controlled. To speed up the movement, simply move the lever towards the **"F"**. To slow down, move the lever towards the **"S"**. Keep in mind many watches have a **+** or **−** symbol instead of letters. You will want to use a small tool for this job, like a toothpick. **Be very careful not to touch the balance spring, or balance spring stud. The spring can easily be damaged.** Often moving the regulator lever is referred to as adjusting the watch's time. *Regulating* actually describes adjusting the watch for consistency, so the watch runs + or − the same amount of seconds per day. But most people use the term *"regulate"* when talking about speeding up or slowing down the movement. *Note: if you own a very expensive watch, like a Rolex or Patek Philippe, then it will probably not have a regulator lever, and will require additional tools to regulate. You should always have professionals work on valuable watches.*

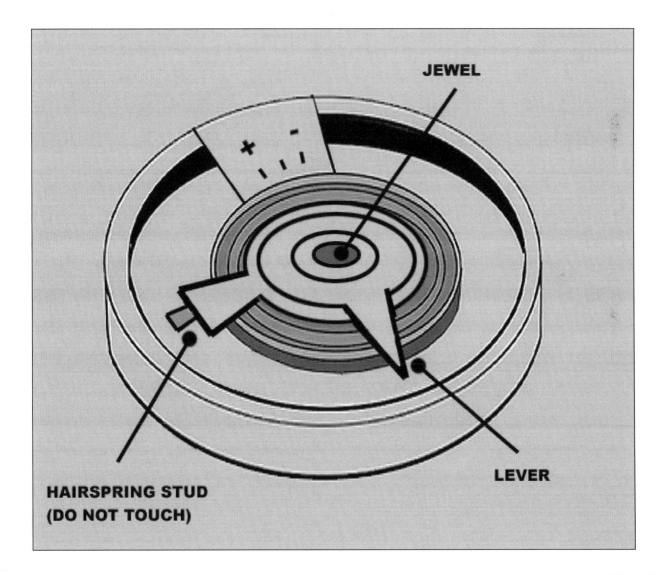

JEWEL

HAIRSPRING STUD
(DO NOT TOUCH)

LEVER

Keep in mind that the opposite end of the regulator lever is your pointer. In the diagram below, the watch was speed up by moving the pointer to the left, towards the "+" sign. The long lever on the opposite end was moved to the right. Many watches do not have an area marked for the pointer. Think of it as the opposite end of the lever, closest to the speed markings (+ or -). **Note: do not touch the hairspring stud (balance spring stud). This will mess up your beats per hour setting, causing the "ticks" and the "tocks" to be different intervals of time. Also be sure not to touch the thin balance spring. It can be damaged quite easily.** The process of adjusting the time will take some trial and error. Adjust it a tiny bit, and then check for accuracy with an accurate clock over the next few hours. Adjust some more and repeat. It could take a few days before you have the watch dialled in to + or – a few seconds per day. If your watch is averaging +6 to -4 seconds per day, then it is extremely accurate, and it is similar to a chronometer watch in one position. A certified chronometer must maintain this average for 15 days in 5 different positions, and at varying temperatures and water depths. Keep in mind that +/- 60 seconds per day is normal for a vintage watch. And a speed of +/- 10 seconds per day is also normal for a new mechanical watch.

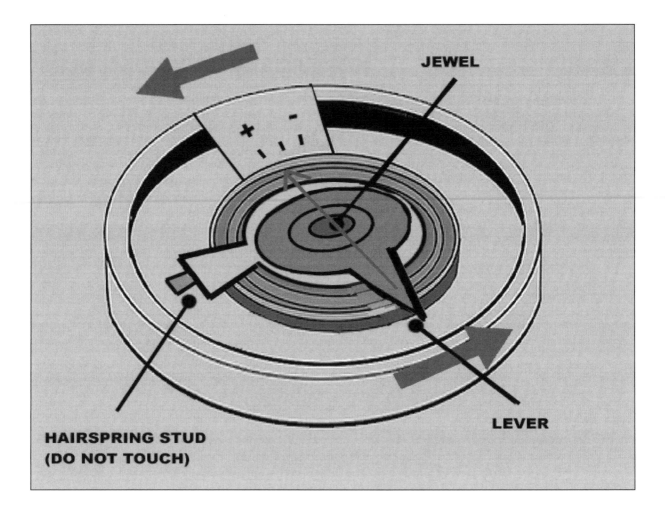

Inside the red circle below you will see the balance, regulator lever, and balance spring stud. Remember, do not touch the balance spring, or balance spring stud!

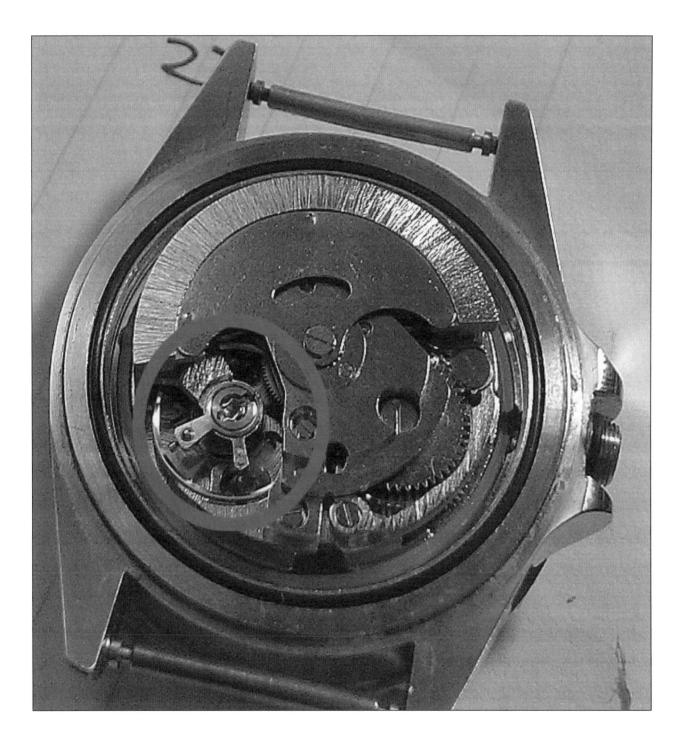

This Chinese watch movement has the words fast and slow etched into the plate.

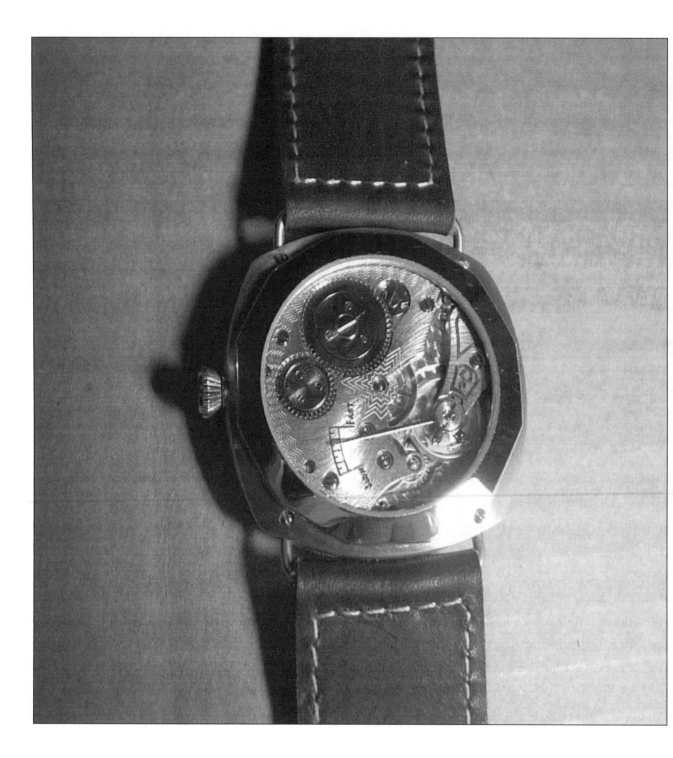

Some of the Chinese made pilot watches by Ticino and Parnis come with a glass case back, which offers a great view of the jewels, balance, ratchet, and crown wheel.

A Chinese made pilot watch with the second hand at 6:00.

In this example, there is a visible pointer that directs the regulator towards the + and − sign. You are less likely to touch the balance spring by accident when adjusting this movement.

DATE WHEEL   Some watches will have a rotating wheel that tells the date, or day of the month (number). If you have a day wheel, it will tell you the day of the week (Sunday-Saturday). The example below shows a Miyota quartz movement with both wheels.

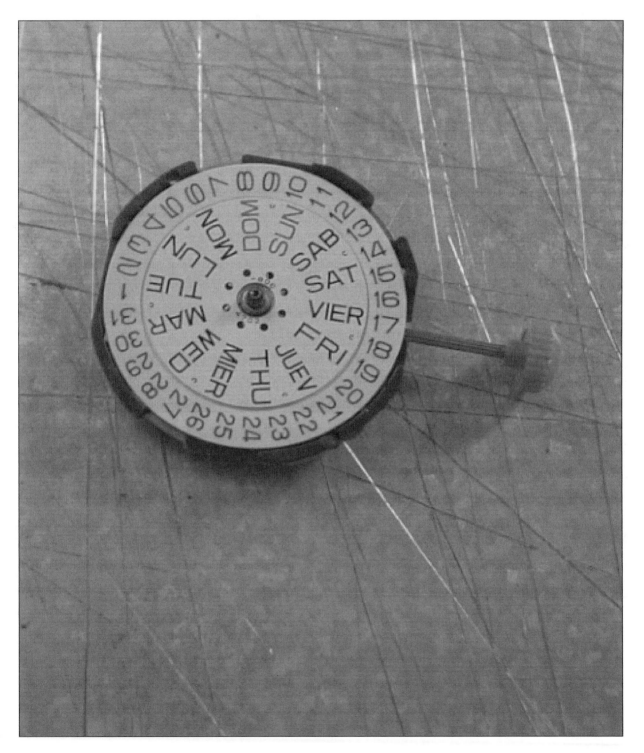

97

QUARTZ This common earth mineral is also known as silicon dioxide. It basically replaces the balance in a mechanical watch. Here is how it works. When a battery sends a small electrical charge to a paper thin quartz crystal, it vibrates, or "oscillates", at a constant frequency of 32,768 times per second. This energy is transformed into electrical impulses via a microchip, which converts the impulses into mechanical energy thanks to a stepping motor. This motor then sends energy to the watch gears, causing the watch hands to move and tell the time.

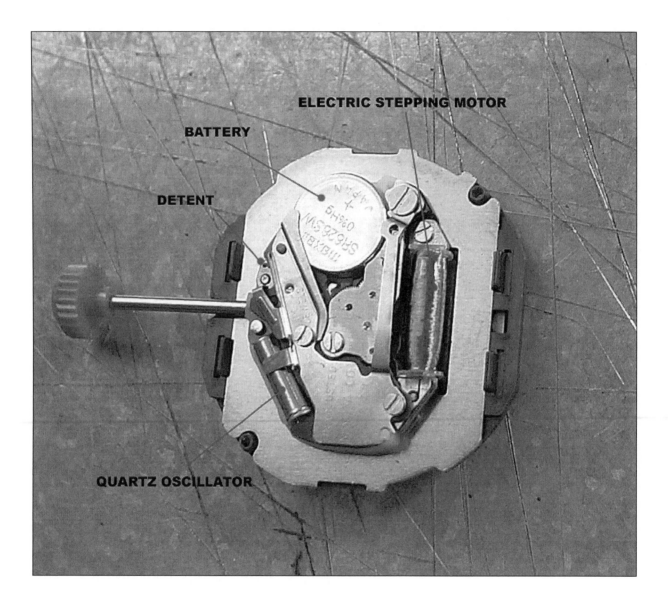

DIAL FEET Dial feet are the two small metal tabs that extend out of the back of the watch dial. These tabs fit into two holes located in the watch movement. This helps keep the dial and movement stationary.

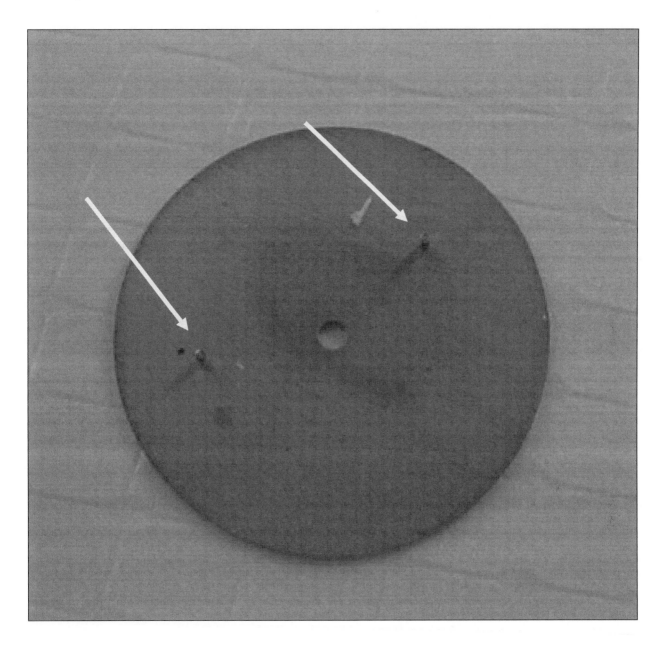

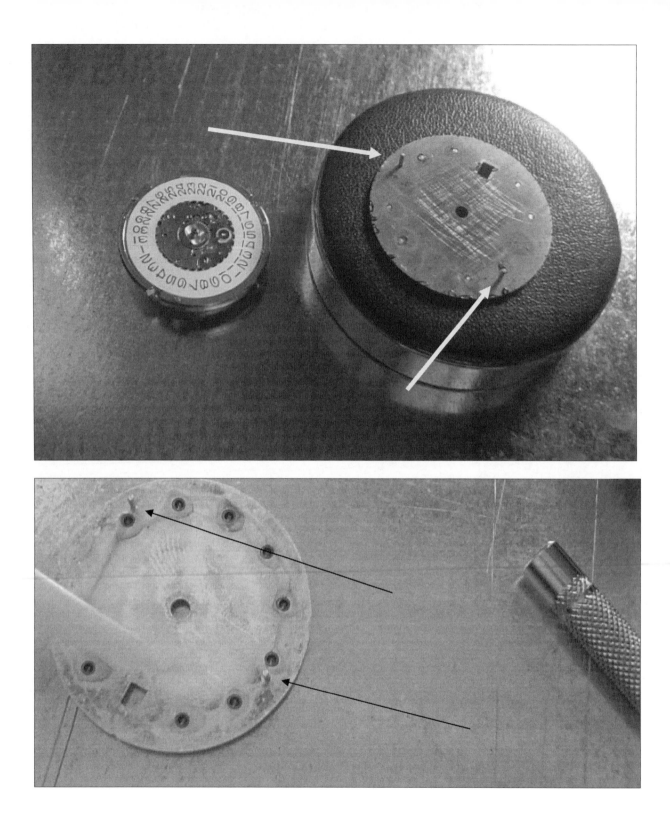

Here is an ETA 805.114 movement and holder. Notice the holes for the dial feet.

WATCH TOOLS

Now that you have a very basic understanding of how a watch works, let's take a look at some of the tools that you might need to purchase in order to build a watch. All of these items are readily available, and many can be found on Ebay under the search term "watch tool kit". A new tool set can cost you as little as $10 with free shipping, and as much as a few hundred dollars for a professional set. It all depends on how much money you want to spend. You can also buy each of the items individually, since you will probably not need every tool that comes in a watch tool set. Below are some of my favorite sites for buying watch making tools.

http://www.ebay.com

http://www.esslinger.com/Watchrepairtools.aspx

http://www.ofrei.com/page235.html

PLIERS AND WIRE CUTTERS

You probably already have these tools in your garage somewhere. Everybody needs a good pair of wire cutters and pliers for cutting and grabbing. Specifically, the wire cutters will be used for cutting stems to the appropriate length. You can find these at any hardware store and most grocery stores.

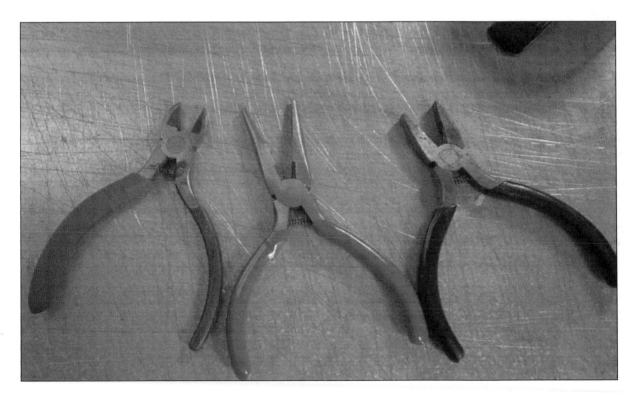

SPRING BAR TOOL

This tool is needed for adding and removing watch bands and bracelets. The spring bar tool works by grabbing a hold of the notches in the spring bar, which allow you to compress the spring bars so they can be pulled out of the watch case lug holes.

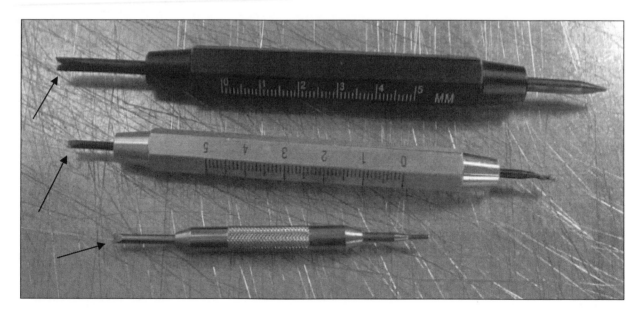

The small fork end on the spring bar tool is used to compress the spring bar, allowing the spring bar to move in and out of the watch case lug holes when changing the band.

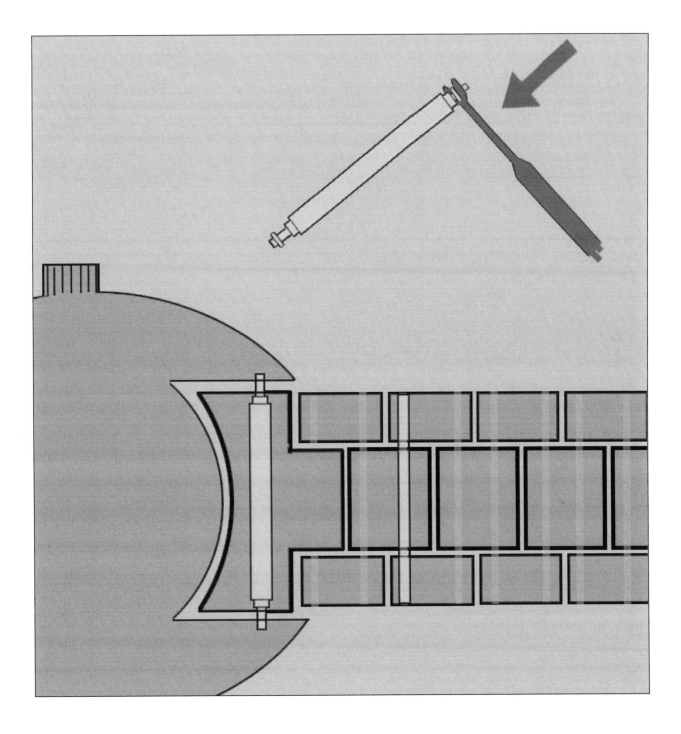

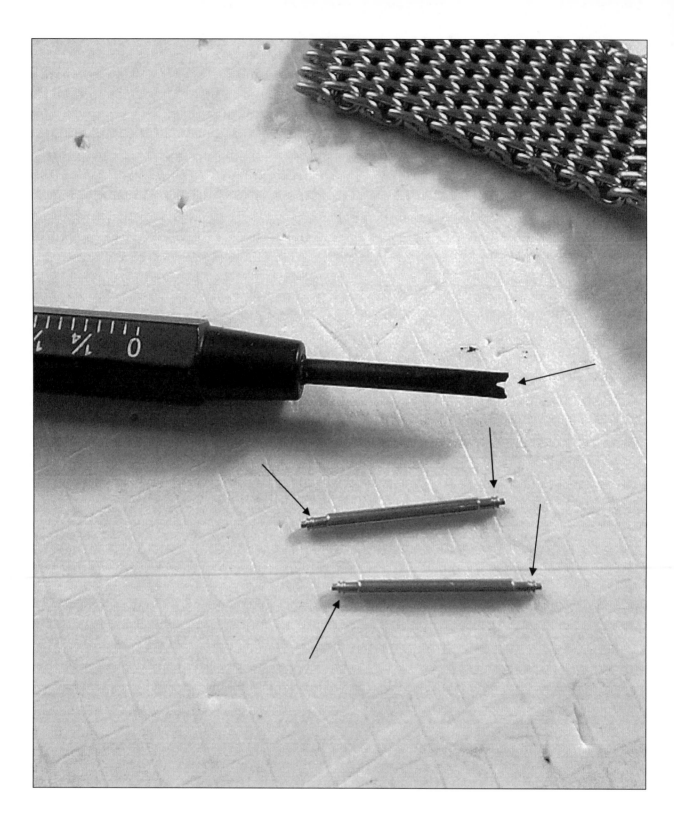

TWEEZERS

A good pair of tweezers is essential for grasping the watch hands and attaching them to a movement. This is one tool that will get a lot of use, so don't skimp on these. Get a high quality set of metal tweezers from www.ofrei.com or www.esslinger.com.

Make sure your tweezers are flat on the tips so that they can grab small watch parts with ease. If the ends are bent outwards and don't touch one another, bend them back down with pliers, or file off the damaged parts.

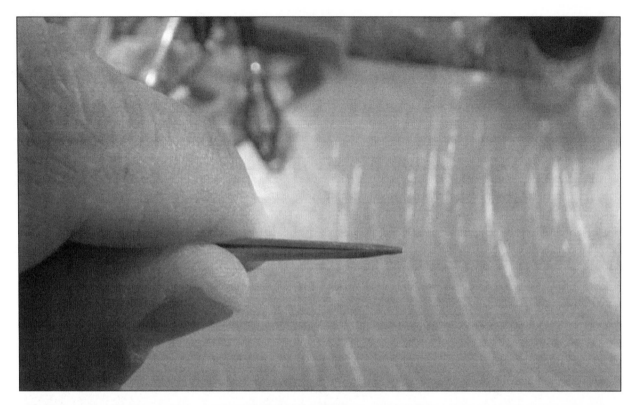

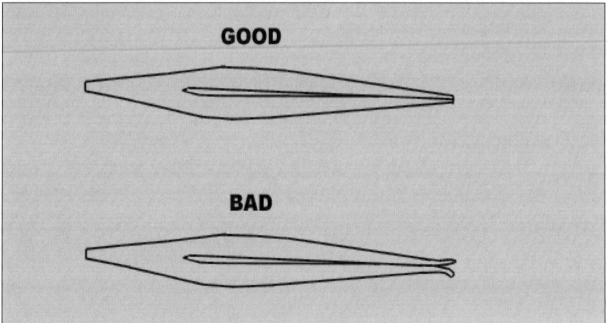

CASE OPENERS

There are three main types of case backs available on watches: the screw-on case back, the Rolex-style case back, and the snap-on case back. Each type of case back requires a different tool for installation. Luckily, many watch tool sets include two or three of these styles. Pictured below is a case knife. It is used for prying off a snap-on watch case back, which is not waterproof. You can use a pocket knife blade instead of a case knife, but you have to be very careful not to scratch the case when using a sharp blade.

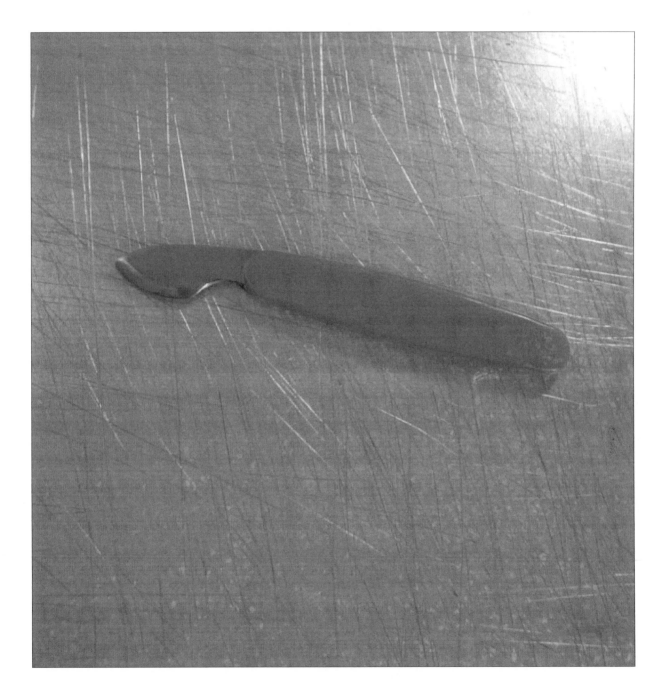

Here are some case openers for waterproof screw-on case backs. The pink HORB ball is used for opening Rolex style case backs with teeth around the case back perimeter. When pressed against the case back, the ball sticks to the metal teeth and is able to twist off the case. The other two case openers pictured below have special adjustable pins which allow you to open screw-on case backs. These openers usually come with a set of round, square, and flat pins. These pins fit into the notches on the case back, allowing you to loosen or tighten the case back.

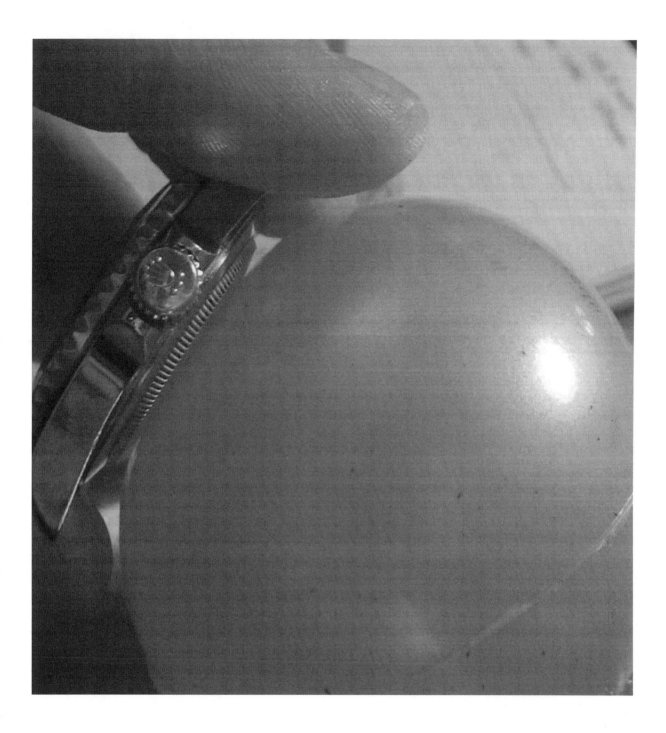

Here is a special tool for opening Rolex style case backs with teeth on them. These cost around $20, but can be priced as high as $200, depending on the model you buy. Look on Ebay for the cheaper versions.

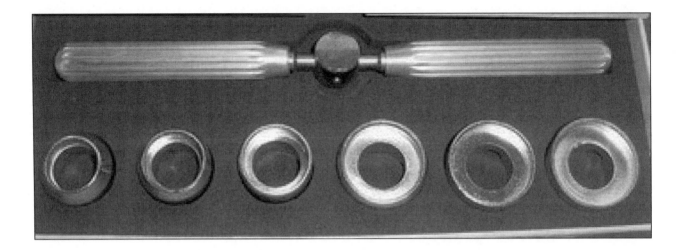

Here are the three types of watch case backs. The one on the far left is a snap-on case back, which gets pried off and pressed back on. The middle one is a typical screw-on case back with notches. The far right one is a Rolex-style case back with teeth.

Here is the Rolex-style case back.

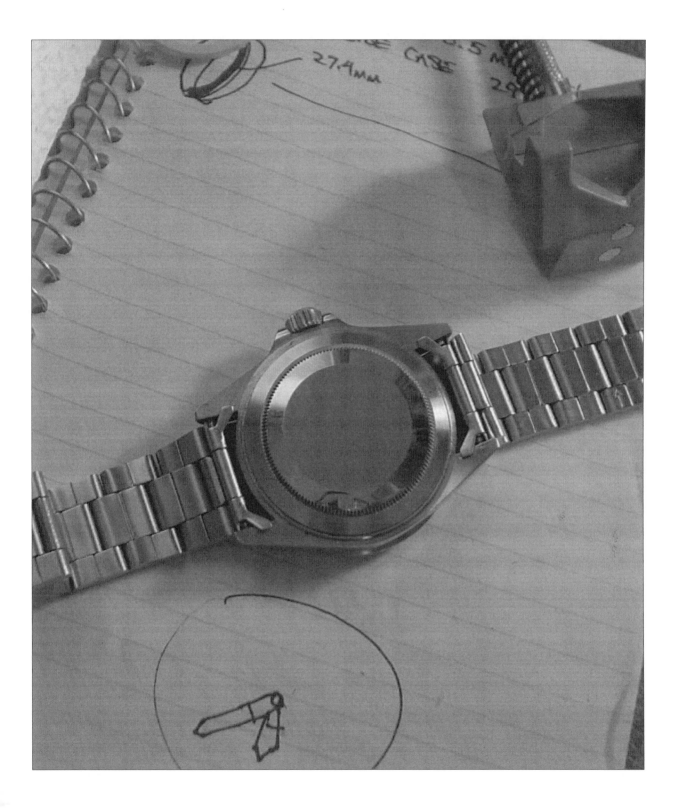

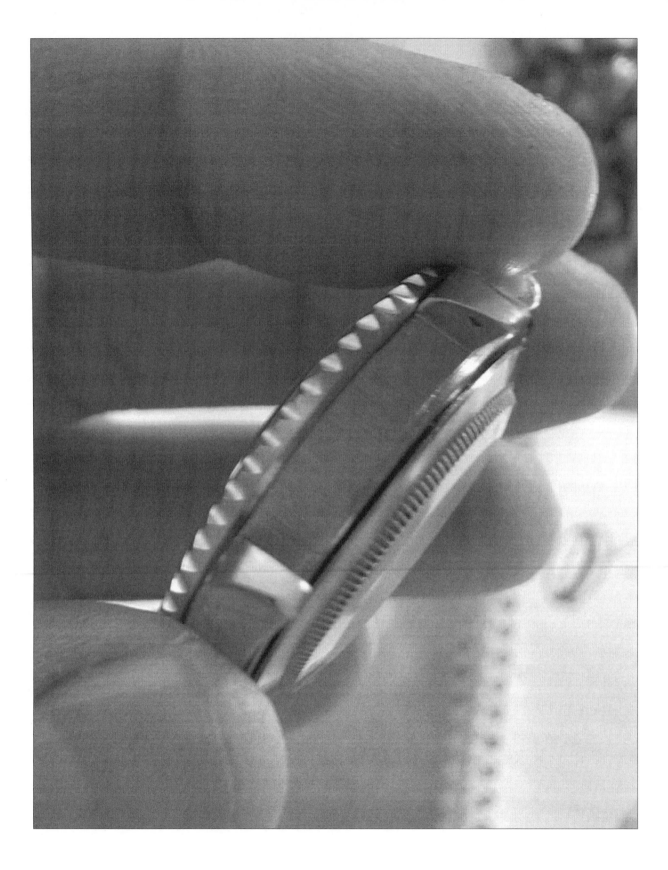

Here is an actual Rolex Submariner 16040 case back.

Here is the front of the watch.

Take a look at the snap-on style case back. Find the groove in the case back and insert the knife blade. Now just pry off the case back.

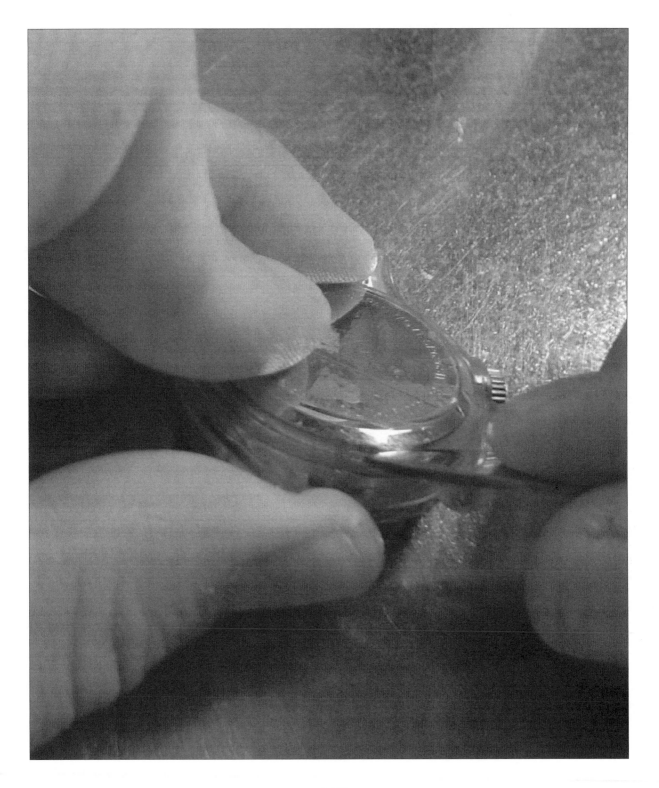

Here is another pic. See the groove?

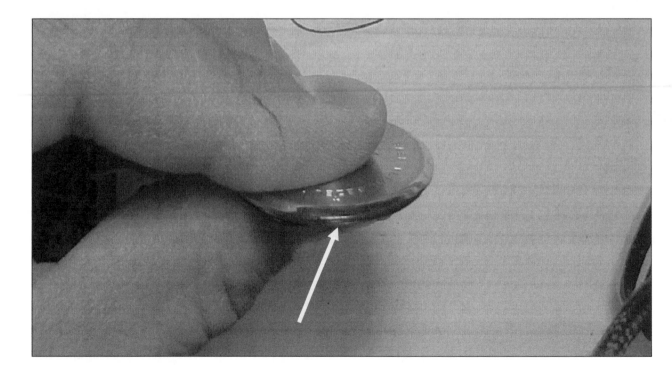

Below is the screw on case back with notches.

Here is the adjustable case back opener in action.

I like to add duct tape to my bench vise, and then use it to hold watches when removing the case backs. Not only does it make the task much easier, but it also helps prevent the case back opener from slipping. Slippage on a watch usually equates to a scratched up case. Not good.

The snap-on case back requires a case knife to open the watch. The other two case backs require a case opener in order for them to be removed from the watch case.

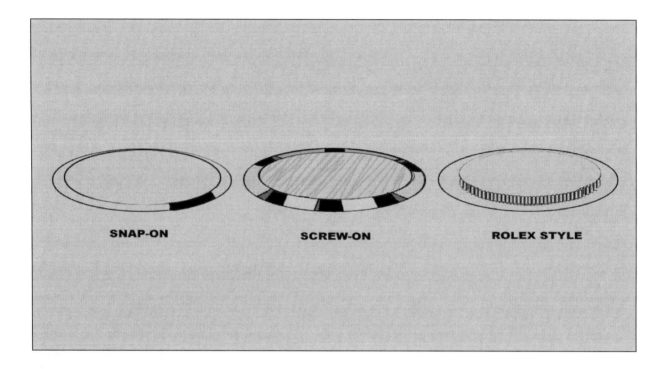

SNAP-ON   SCREW-ON   ROLEX STYLE

POCKET KNIFE

A pocket knife with a thin blade is a perfect tool for popping off a watch bezel or case back. Feel free to add duct tape to the area you are working on in order to prevent the knife from slipping and scratching the watch case.

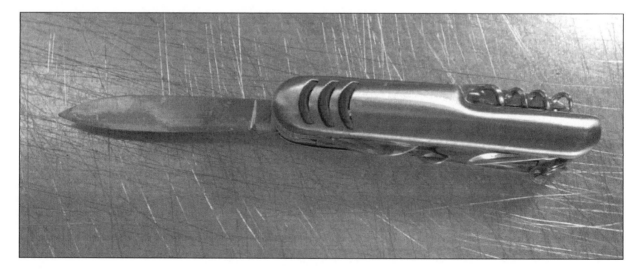

A thin blade is needed for the job. Simply pry off the bezel with your knife.

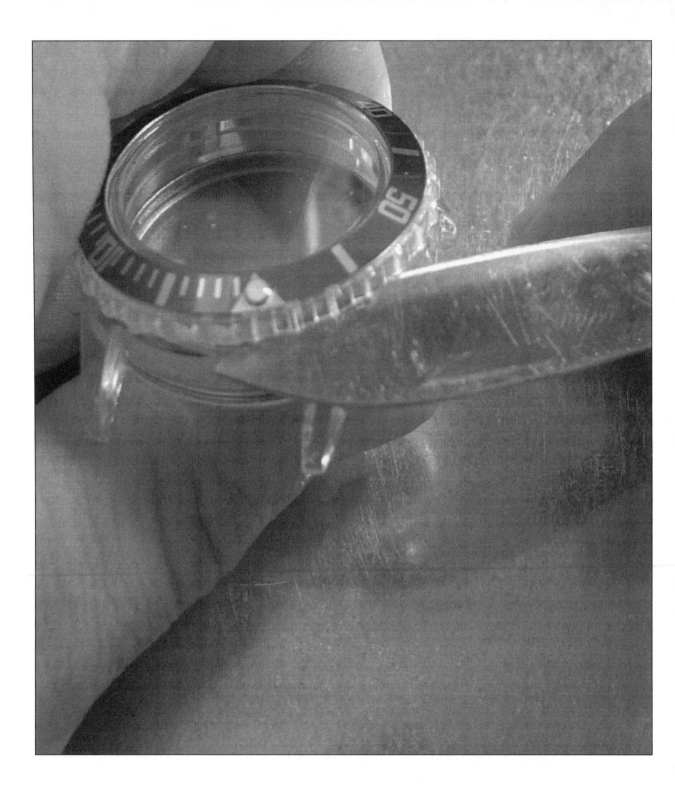

There are a bunch of teeth on the back side of the bezel. A spring fits underneath the bezel. It allows the bezel to move in one direction small increments. Bezels not used for diving often move in both directions and are uni-directional.

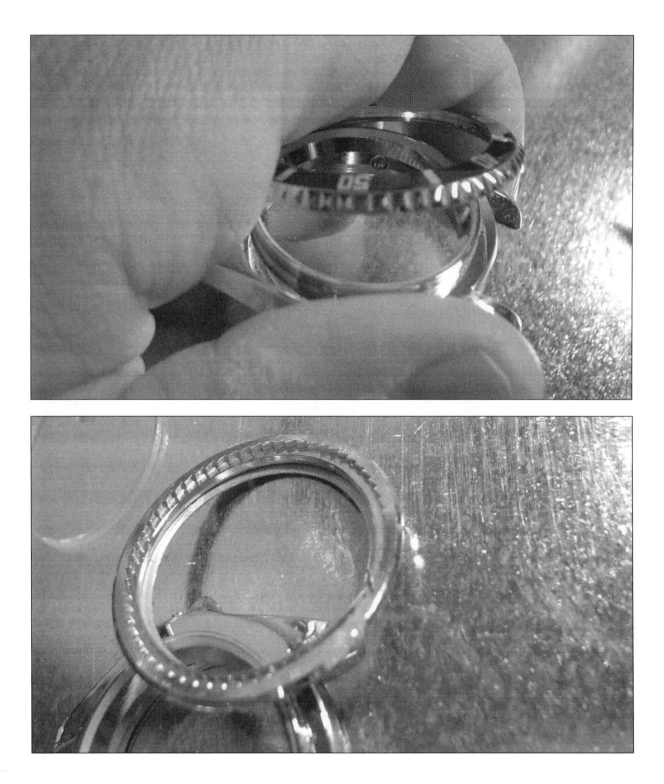

So how do you use a rotating bezel? Let's say you are going on a dive. The time is 7:15. You rotate the bezel to the 0 setting. Now the bezel is now next to the 15 minute mark. If you look at the minute hand, you will know how long you have been diving for. For example, at 7:25 you will have been diving for 10 minutes. At 7:35 you will have been diving for 20 minutes.

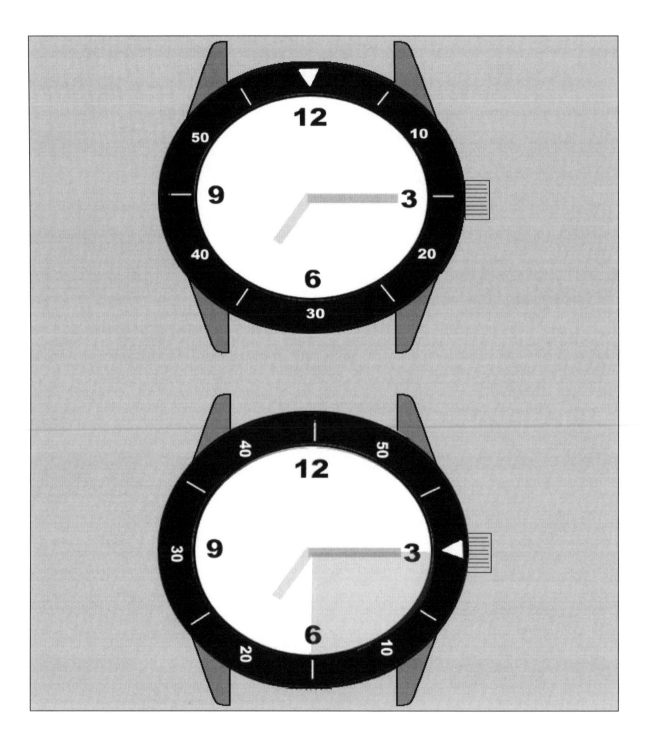

Here is the spring. It fits into a hole in the watch case.

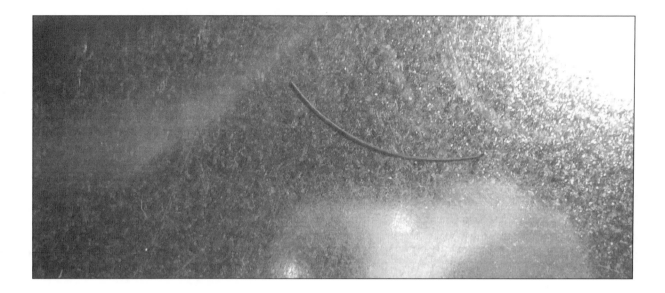

You can use your fingers to push the bezel insert off of the bezel. It is usually stuck to the bezel with some type of adhesive. To change the insert, simply place some glue on the backside of the new insert and press the it back on the bezel.

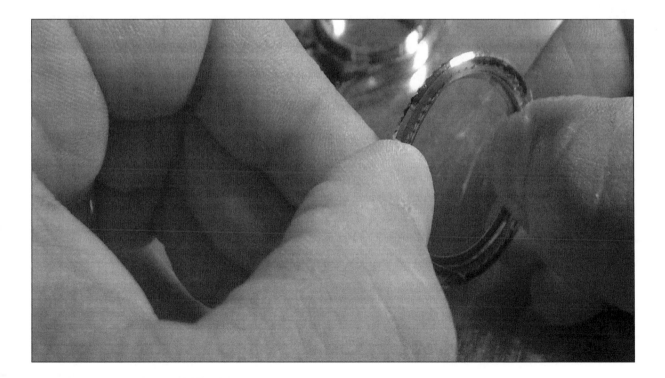

In the diagram below, you can see how bezel only moves in one direction because the spring is constantly pushing to the left, causing it to engage with the bezel teeth.

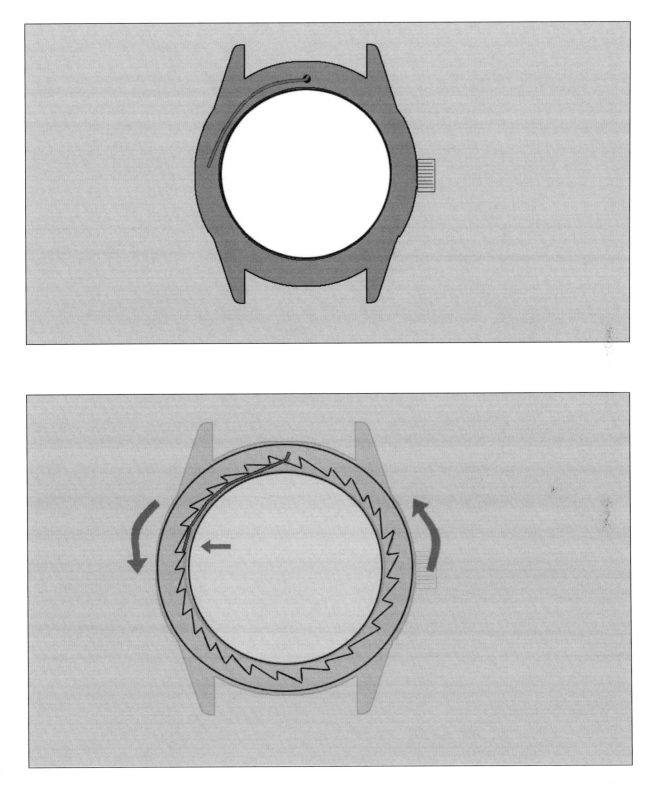

To reinstall the bezel, you need to engage the spring with one of the bezel teeth. Then rotate the bezel counter clockwise a little bit, press down on the bezel, and pop it back on the watch case.

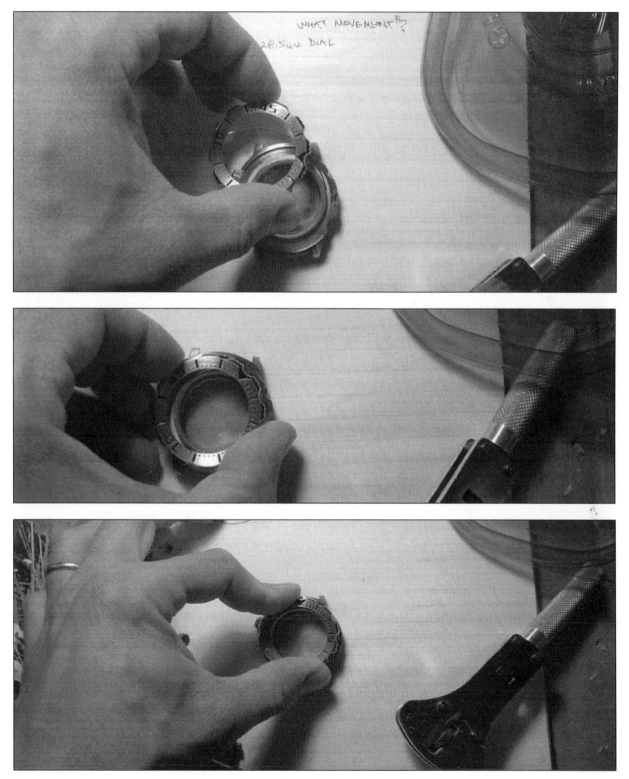

Now you can install a new bezel insert. Remove any old glue residue from the watch case. Then add a small amount of glue to the back of the new insert, and press it onto the bezel.

On more expensive watches, the spring is actually a thin ring that sits underneath the bezel. These are very easy to work with. Simply pop off the bezel with a knife and press it back on when you are ready to reinstall it. The spring pictured below several small lugs that fit into small holes in the watch case.

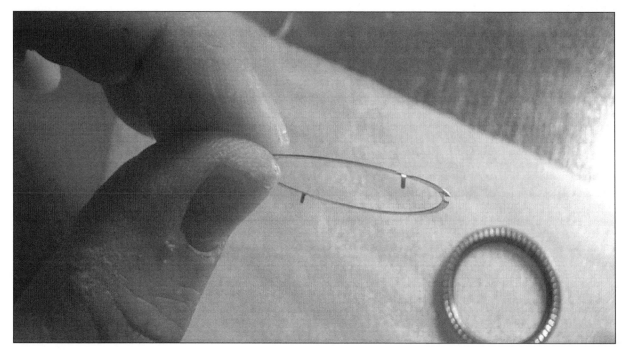

Make sure the spring is on and press the bezel back on. The Seiko Diver pictured below was found on Ebay under the key words "sample watch." Sometimes you can get a great deal on new parts by using those keywords in a search.

LOUPE

Many of the watch parts you will be dealing with are very small. Therefore, a loupe, or jeweler's magnifying glass, is needed in order to see what you are doing, especially when installing watch hands or searching for the movement detent button. I prefer a loupe that comes with a head strap for a hands-free magnification. You can find these for $6 on Ebay.

DIGITAL CALIPER

The digital caliper will answer all of your questions when it comes to sizing. When building a watch from spare parts, measurements are everything. When you know the dimensions of the inside of a watch case, then you will know what parts you can use for your project. Be sure to reset the caliper to "0" before use, and pick up some spare batteries to keep handy in case you leave it on. The Cen-Tech 6" caliper below cost only $10 on Ebay. It uses one 1.5V Maxell LR44 battery.

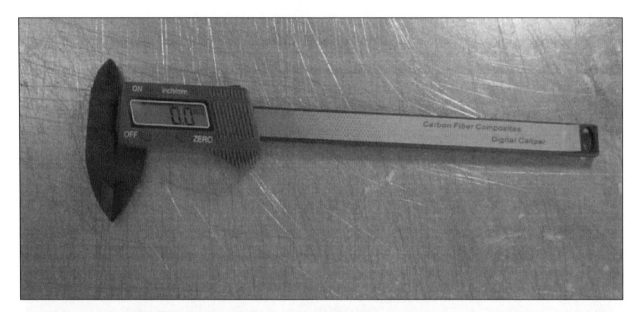

136

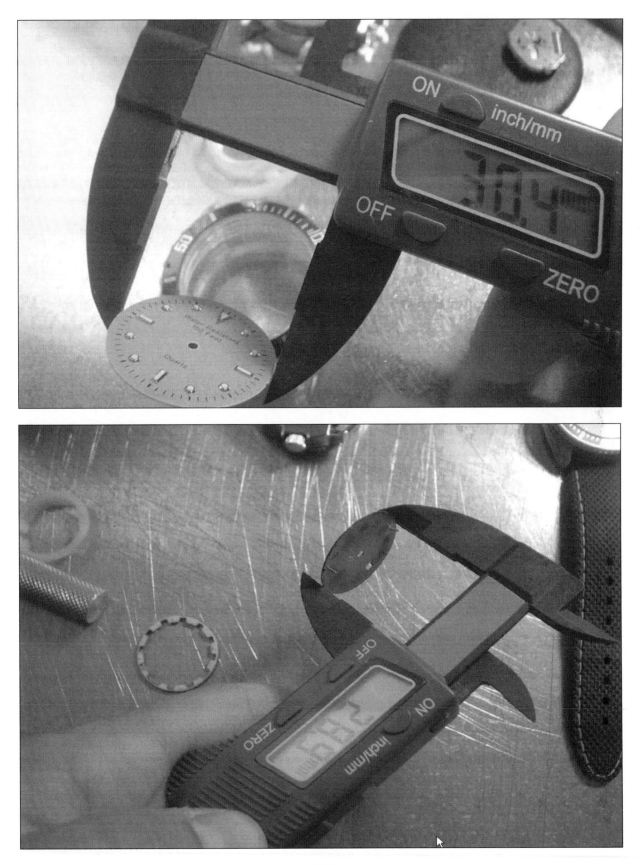

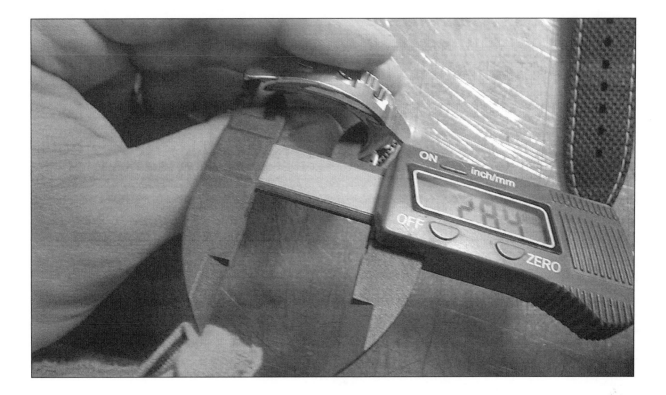

CASE CUSHION (OPTIONAL)

You need some type of clean, particle free surface to place your movement on when you are working on your watch. The case cushion below is perfect for flipping the watch over so you can lift the case off of the movement. Esslinger.com has these cushions for $9.

POLISHING CLOTH

There is no way to avoid it, the watch crystal is going to get dirty, so a good set of polishing cloths are essential. The last thing you want to notice is a smudge on the inside of the crystal after you have screwed on the case back. These cost $2 on Ebay.

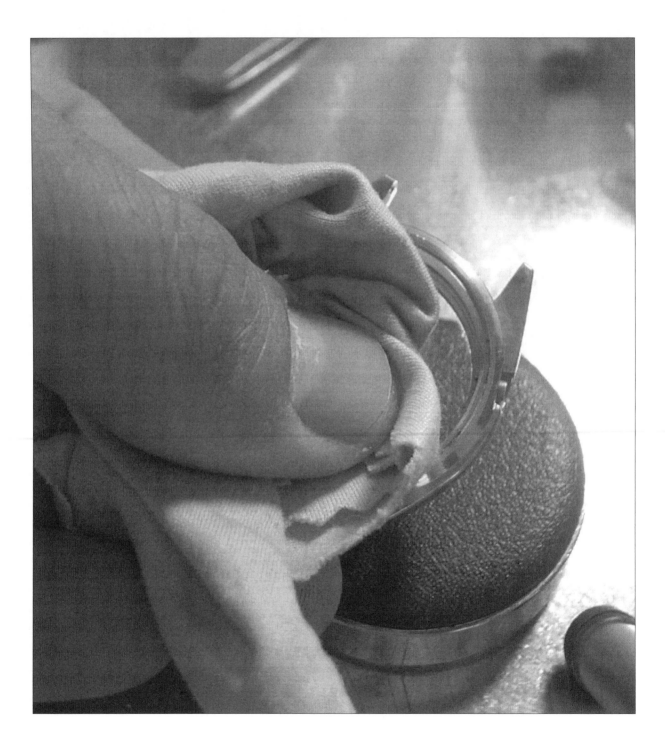

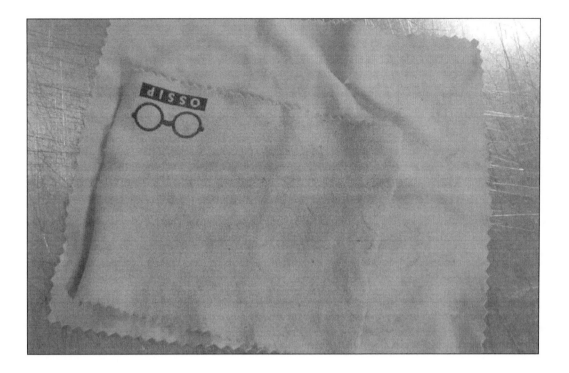

TOOTH PICKS   (OPTIONAL)

I like to use tooth picks when adjusting the angle and position of the watch hands. Metal tools can scratch the watch dial too easily. A box of these cost around $1 at the local grocery store.

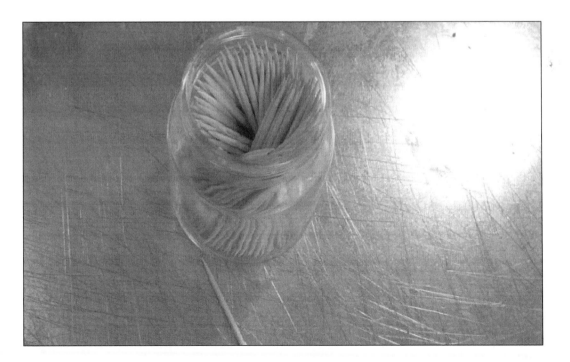

DENTAL PICK   (OPTIONAL)

This is a very handy tool to have around for all kinds of projects. A dental pick or metal pick with a sharp point is perfect for pushing in the movement detent button, and for lifting the watch movement out of the case. A dental pick can also be used for cleaning. It does an excellent job of scraping the dirt off of the case threads.

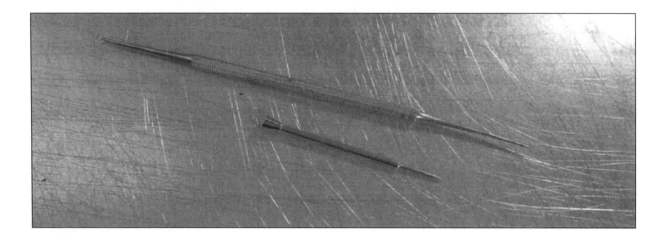

HAND REMOVER

The hand remover is a special tool is used to pull the hands off of the watch movement. This is one of your most important tools, so get a quality hand remover. As you can see below, there are several types of hand pullers available. *Note: another type of hand remover, lever hand removers, can also be used to remove watch hands. In this book we will focus on the movers below because they are cheap and very easy to use.*

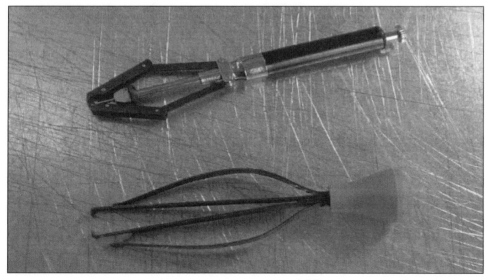

Basically, both of these hand pullers work the same way, when compressed, they grip the watch hands with their arms, lift them upward, and pull them off of the watch movement. In the example below, when the top Presto style puller is squeezed, its arms will lift up the watch hands. I especially like using the Presto puller when the watch hands are positioned close to the watch dial. The lower pantograph style puller has a knob that is pushed down to open up its arms. After opening the arms, just push the hand puller down against the watch dial, and it will grip the hands and lift them up off of the watch movement and dial.

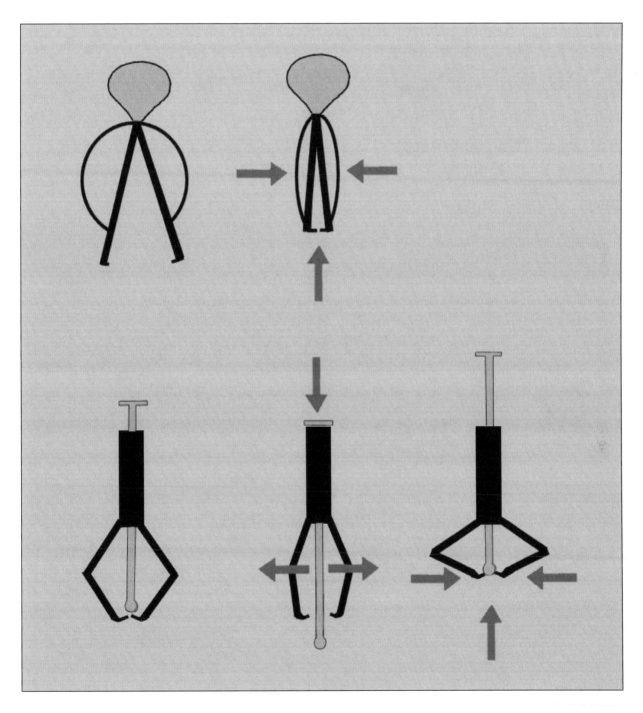

Below is the pantograph style hand remover.

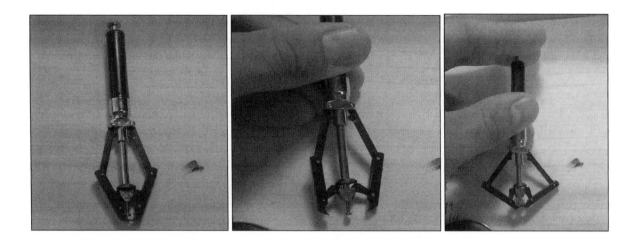

HAND SETTING TOOL

The setting tool is used to press down on the hands when installing them on the watch movement. It is basically a small cylinder with a hole in the middle. You can find these on watch repair websites and also on Ebay for a few bucks.

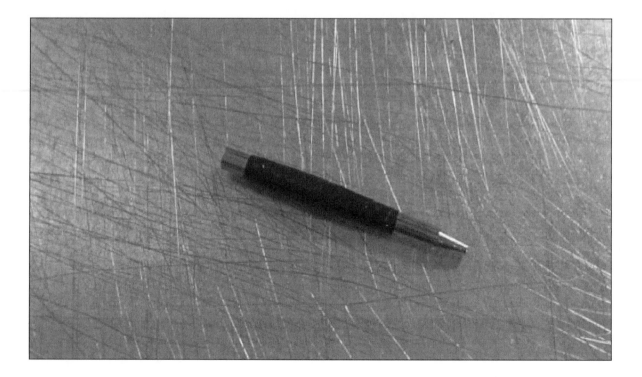

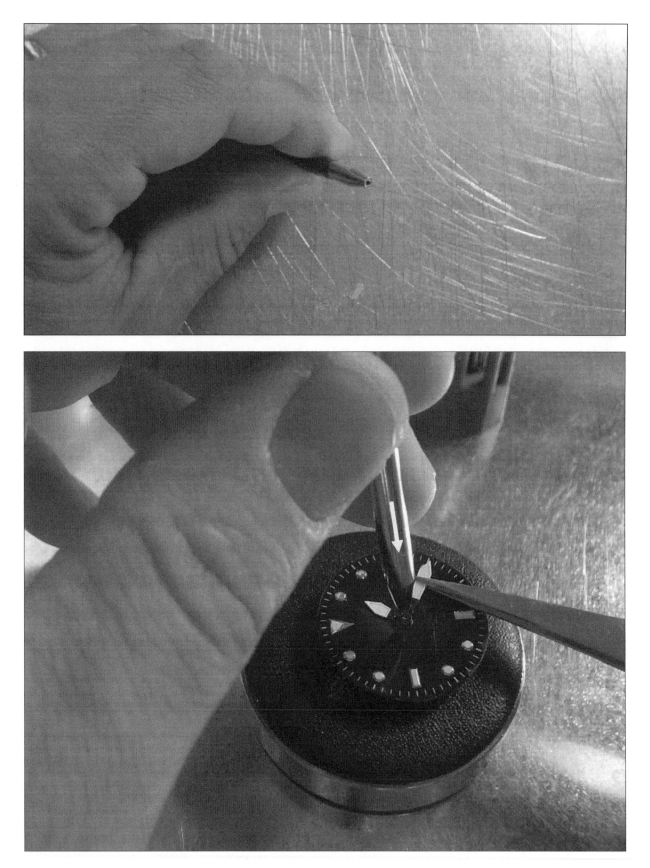

All of the watch hands get installed in the same manner. Hold the hand in position with the tweezers, and then press down with the hand setting tool. This process requires plenty of practice to perfect. Also, keep in the mind that the smaller the hands are, the more difficult the installation will be. It takes more skill to install a 0.17 mm second hand than it would to install a 0.25 mm second hand.

SILCON 7 GREASE

This watch case sealer is perfect for lubricating the case gasket, stem gasket, and case tube. It is a high vacuum pressure sealer that doesn't break down over time, making it perfect for waterproofing your watch. You can find Silcon 7 at www.ofrei.com for around $6.

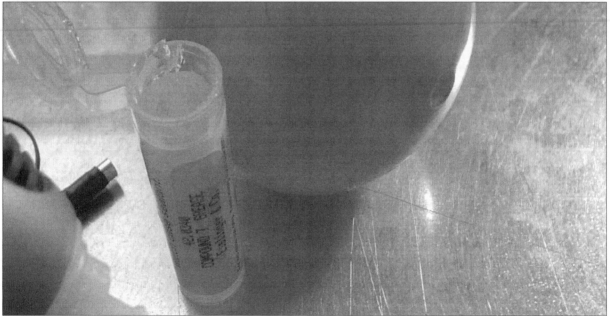

Add Silcon 7 to the case back gasket, case tube, case tube threads, stem threads, and stem gasket.

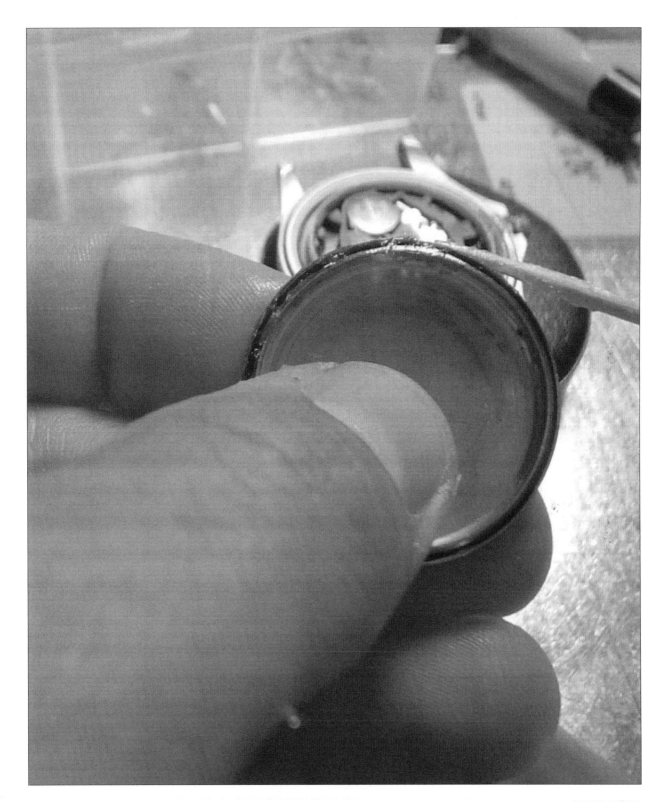

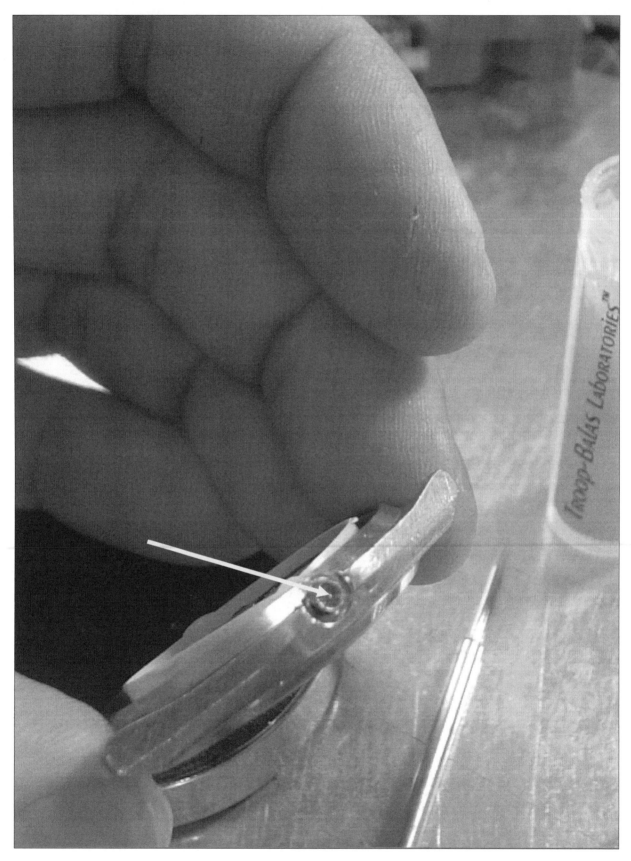

GLUE (OPTIONAL)

There are plenty of glue products on the market that you could use for watch repairs. G-S Hypo Cement is a great choice because it has a precision applicator tip and dries clear. It can be used for attaching crystals to the watch case, or for gluing the dial on to the watch movement for proper positioning before installation. Super glue also makes a glue product designed for glass or plastic watch crystals. The thicker super glue gel can be used for gluing the dial to the sides of the movement if no movement holder is available, or for gluing the crown on to the stem. If you change your mind, the hardened glue can also be removed from the watch case or movement with tweezers or a dental pick. Hypo Cement is available at www.esslinger.com for $5. You can find super glue at any hardware or grocery store.

In the example below, the glue will be used to form a waterproof seal and hold the crystal in place.

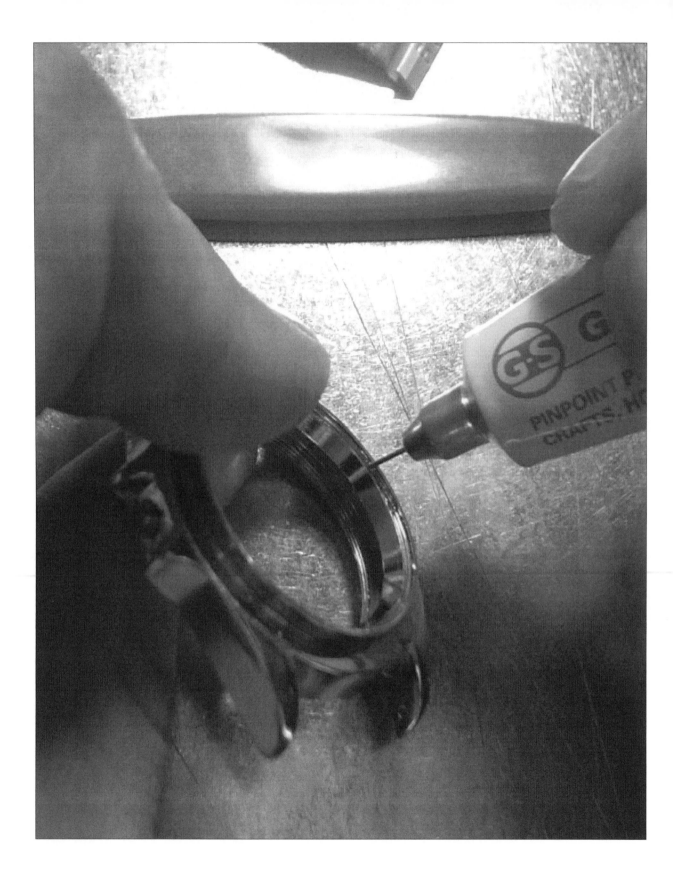

One problem that can occur when using glue is the formation of bubbles. If you end up with visible air bubbles in the glue, you will have to start the process over. Before working on expensive watches, practice gluing in some crystals on cheaper watches.

SCREWDRIVER SET

A good watch, eyeglasses, or jewelry screwdriver set is essential for all types of watch repair. Look for the flat blade type that is small enough for watch repair. The smallest screwdriver should be in the .60mm or .70mm range. You can find these at any of the watch or jewelry repair websites or on Ebay.

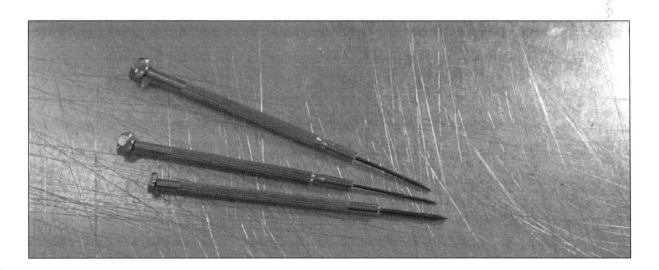

PIN VISE

The pin vise is a small jeweler's tool used to firmly hold small parts, like wires, screws, and bits. Specifically, you will use this vise to cut and hold the watch stem in place while you screw on the crown. These are available online for around $4.

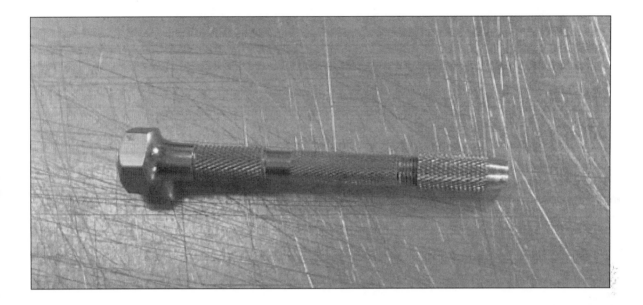

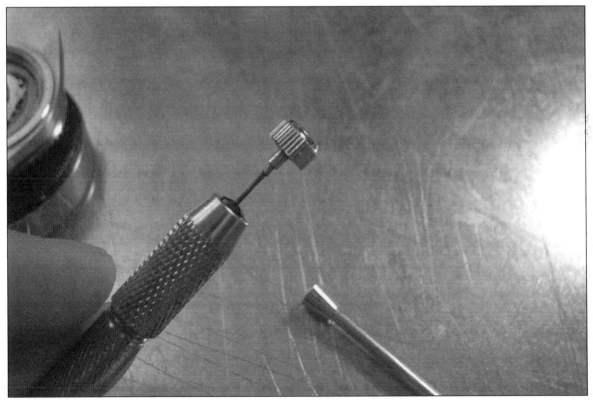

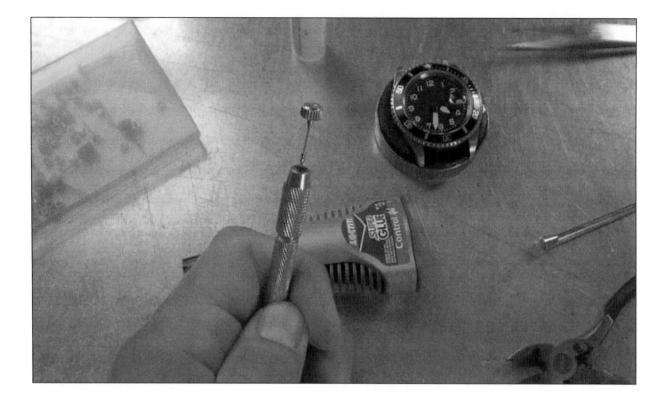

RODICO PUTTY

This amazing sticky green putty will not only clean the fingerprints off of your watch dial, it will also help you pick up some of the smaller watch parts off of your work bench. I use Rodico on every watch project that I carry out. A tube of this stuff cost $5 online.

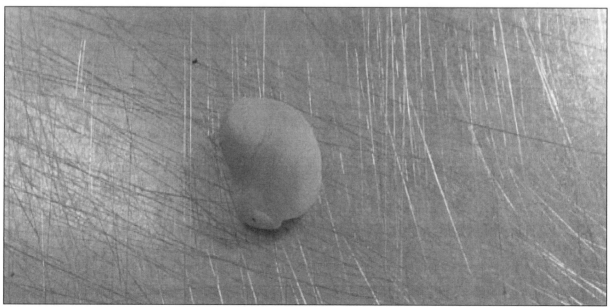

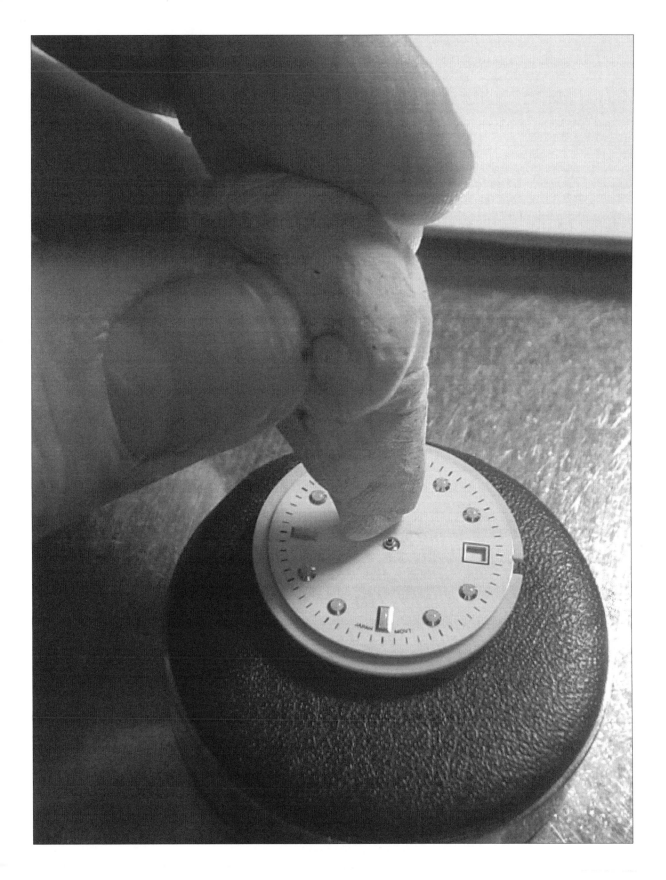

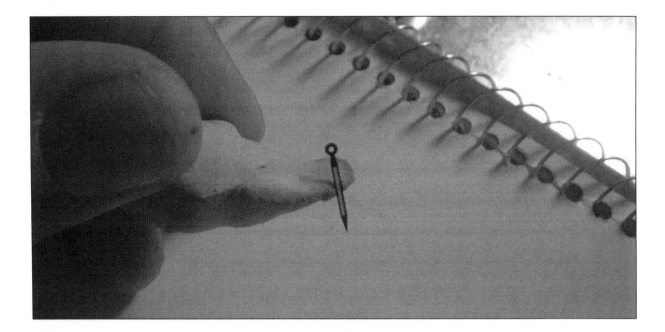

LINK REMOVER   (OPTIONAL)

This tool comes in most watch repair kits. If you need to add or remove links on your metal watch bracelet, then this tool will do the trick. It pushes the pins out that hold the links together. You can also use it to push the pins back in. *Note: The more expensive watch bands use screws to connect the bracelet links together, so you would just need the appropriate screwdriver when working on a high end watch band.*

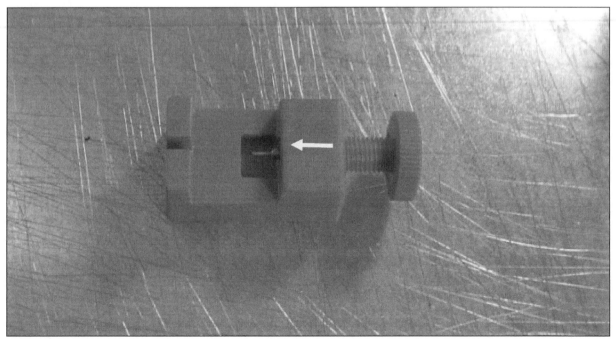

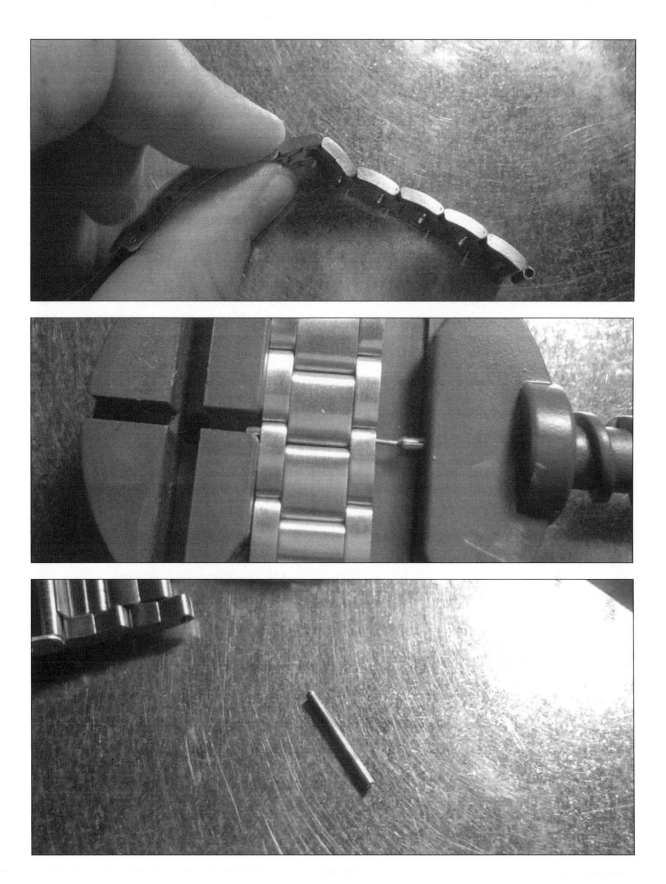

Here is the side view of pretty solid watch bracelet. Notice the holes for the pins.

Can you find the link pins on this watch bracelet?

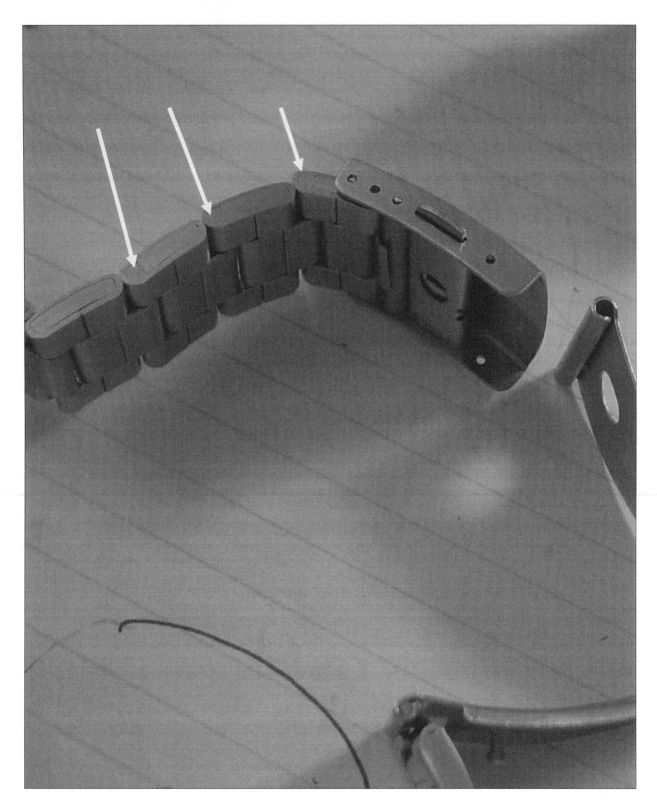

DIAL DOTS (OPTIONAL)

These are small pieces of double sided tape that allow you to maintain the dial's position on top of the movement until it is inserted into the case. These come in handy when you replace the existing watch dial with a new one, and the dial feet on the new dial don't match up with the holes in the movement holder. If that is the case, you can cut off the dial feet with wire cutters, and then use tweezers to place 3-4 dial dots on the movement, away from any moving parts. The last step is to remove the brown paper from the top of the dial dots.

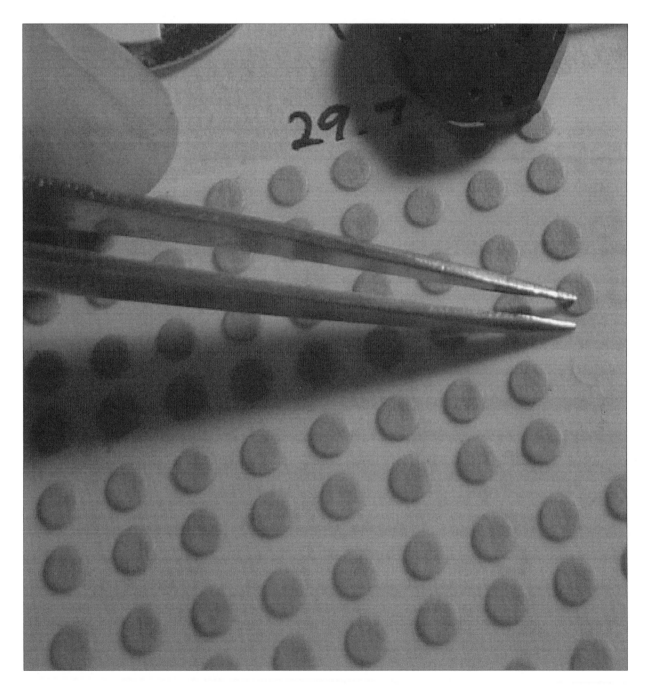

Now the dial is ready to be positioned on top of the movement.

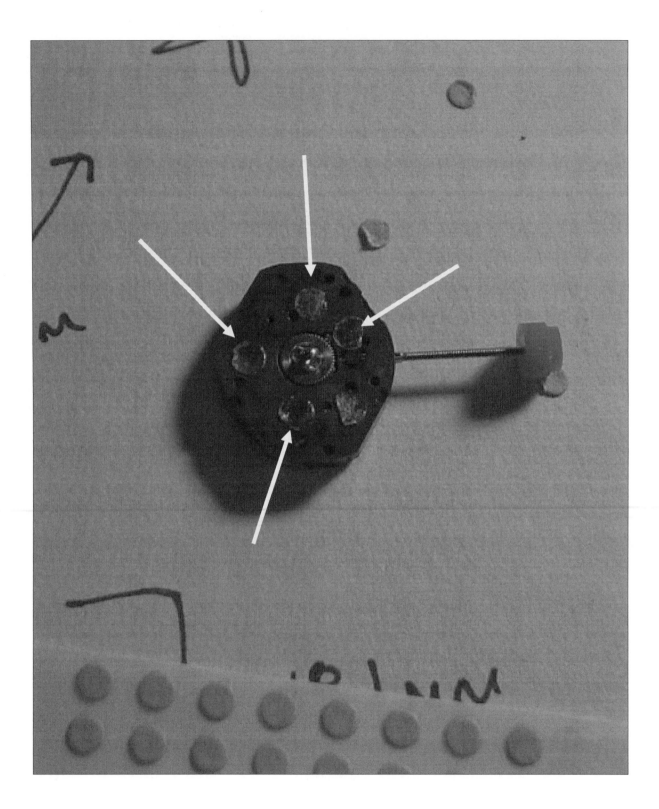

DIAL PROTECTOR

The dial of a watch scratches very easily. So when you are removing the hands from the watch dial, you have to take special care not to scuff up the dial with the hand remover tool. To prevent damage to the watch dial, a plastic dial protector is used. It goes under the hands, and on top of the dial. The protector below is from www.ofrei.com. You can also make your own dial protector out of paper.

CRYSTAL PRESS (OPTIONAL)

The lever style crystal press is used for popping out watch crystals, and pushing them back into the case. *Note: only cases with a friction gasket need a crystal press for installation. A watch without a friction gasket requires glue to hold the crystal in place.* Below is a crystal press from www.ofrei.com that retails for around $35. The press comes with several different sized dies that fit inside different sized cases. This press can also be used to install snap on case backs.

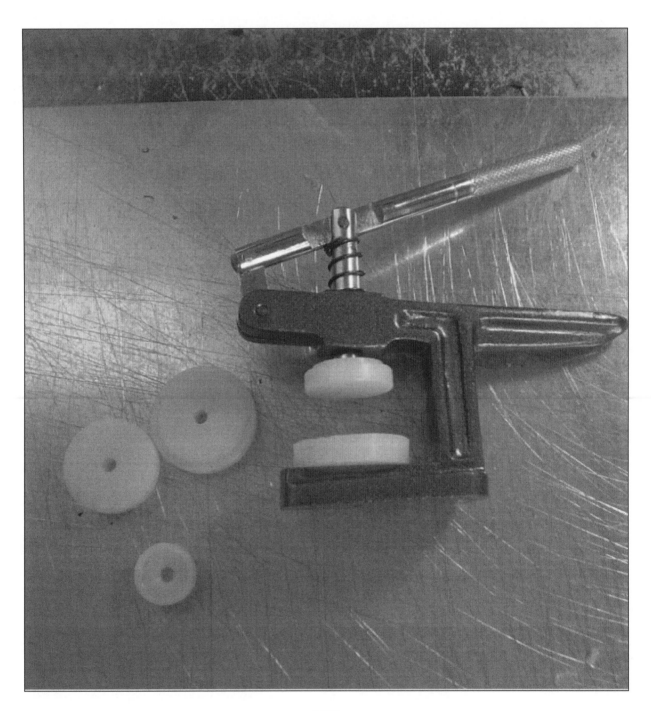

Take a look at the crystal press in action. The crystal below is cracked and needs to be replaced. A smaller die fits inside the case, and a larger die is positioned at the bottom of the crystal press. It is used to hold the case and catch the falling crystal.

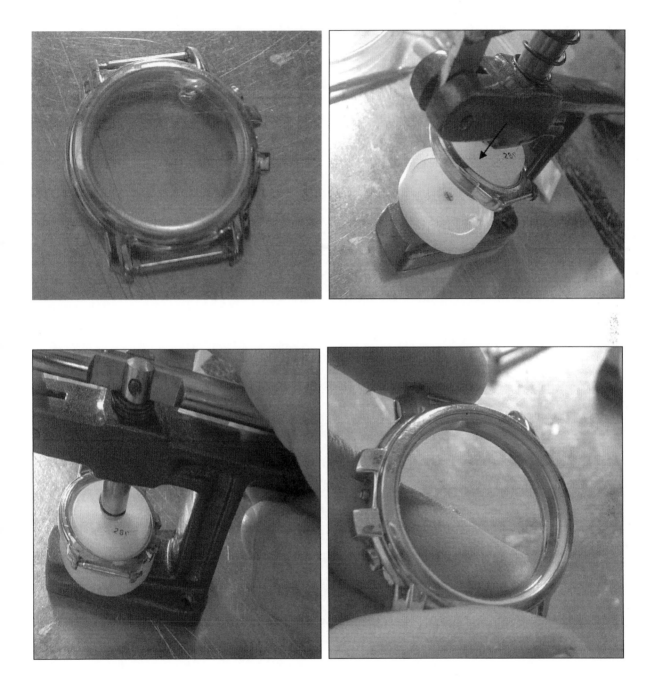

Here is a close up of a friction gasket. Put it in the case along with the new crystal, and press down on the lever. The new crystal is in place.

174

SPEEDI-FIT (OPTIONAL)

This quick dying putty is a type of case filler that is used to create movement holders when the correct size is not available. It is often used when retro-fitting quartz movements, or adding a quartz movement to a watch that has a broken mechanical movement. This method is costly and requires a bit of practice before attempting it on a real project. It cost around $38 at http://www.jewelerssupplies.com. Speedi-fit comes in two containers. Mix equal parts of the orange and white putty together with your hands. Now you have about 20 seconds before it starts to harden, so you need to work fast. Roll out a line of the putty and pack it inside the gaps in the case. *Note: The movement, crown, stem, dial, and hands should already be in position before you mix the Speedi-Fit movement holder.*

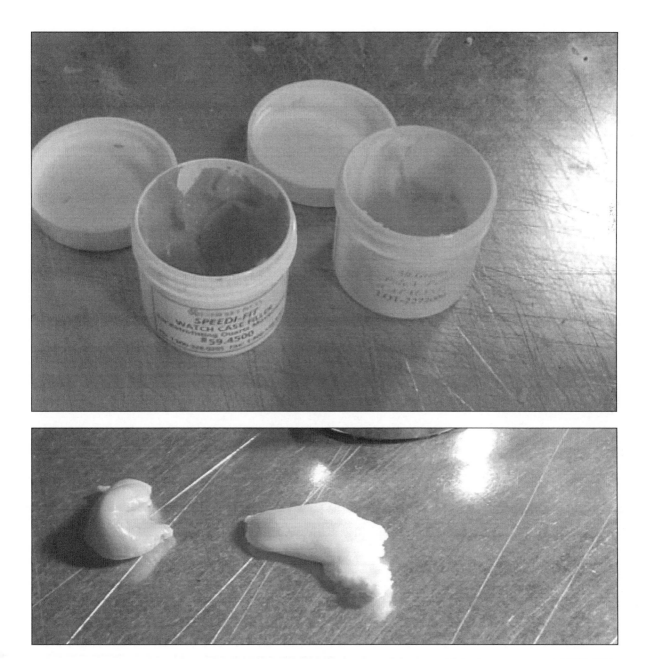

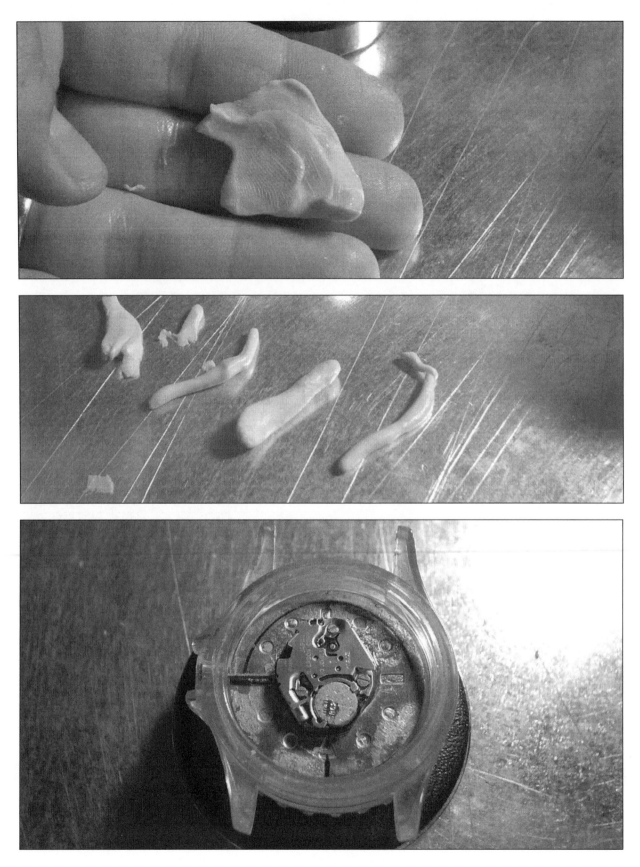

Once the Speedi-fit completely dries (3 minutes) you can shave it down with a razor blade. Be sure to cut a space for the stem.

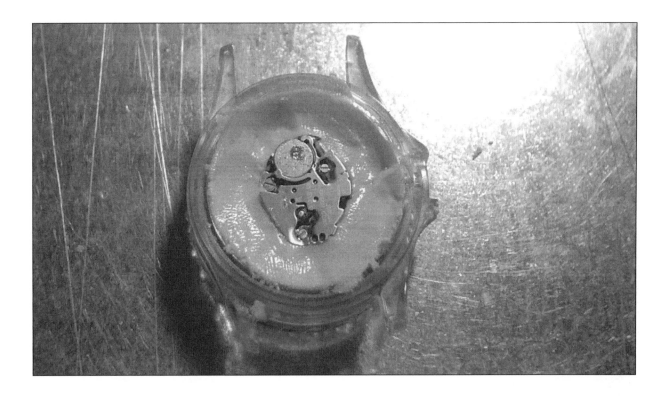

Shave off any excess putty, and cut out a section around the case threads, so you can screw on the case back.

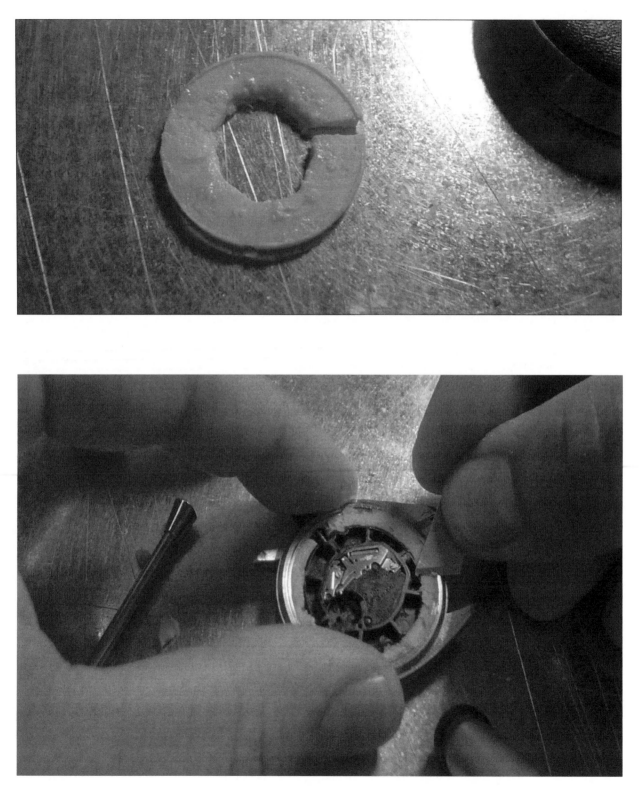

Here is the shape that you want for the Speedi-fit movement holder. You will have to shave off some of the Speedi-fit to make room for the case threads, so that the case back can screw on the case.

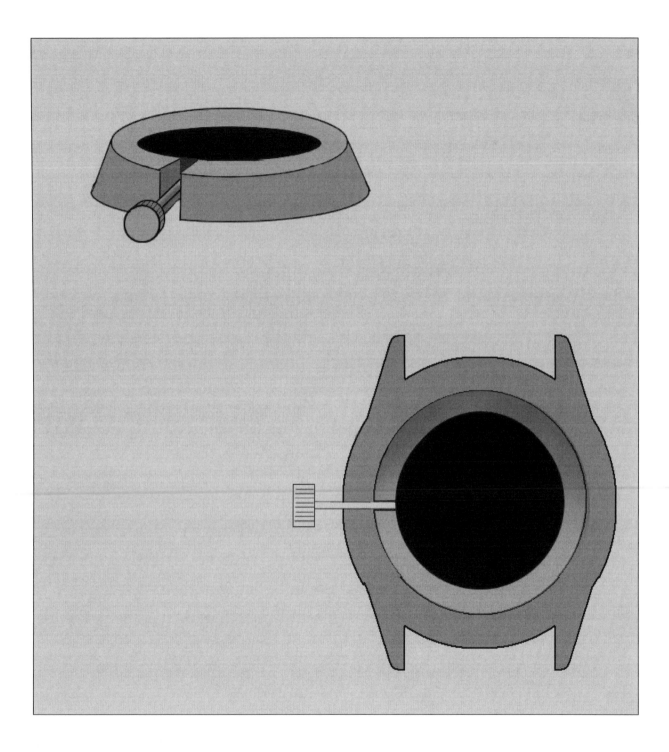

STEM EXTENDERS (OPTIONAL)

When you are switching out a watch movement, you will sometimes find that the new movement has a stem that is too short. The fix is easy. Just get the proper size stem extender, add glue and screw it onto the end of the new stem. Now cut the stem and extender to the proper length. Then add glue and screw on the crown. Esslinger.com sells the stem extender kits for $16.95.

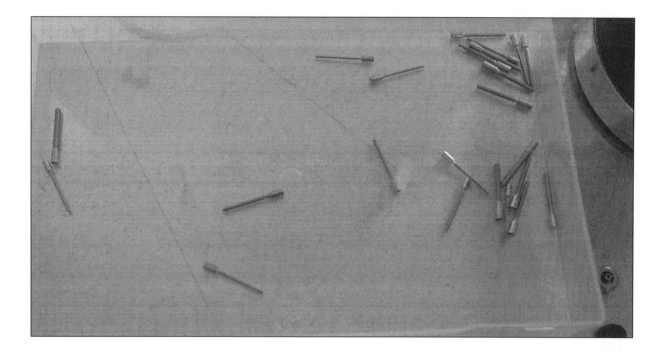

In the picture below, the stem that is being held in the pin vise is too short. Add some loctite or crazy glue, and then screw on the stem extender.

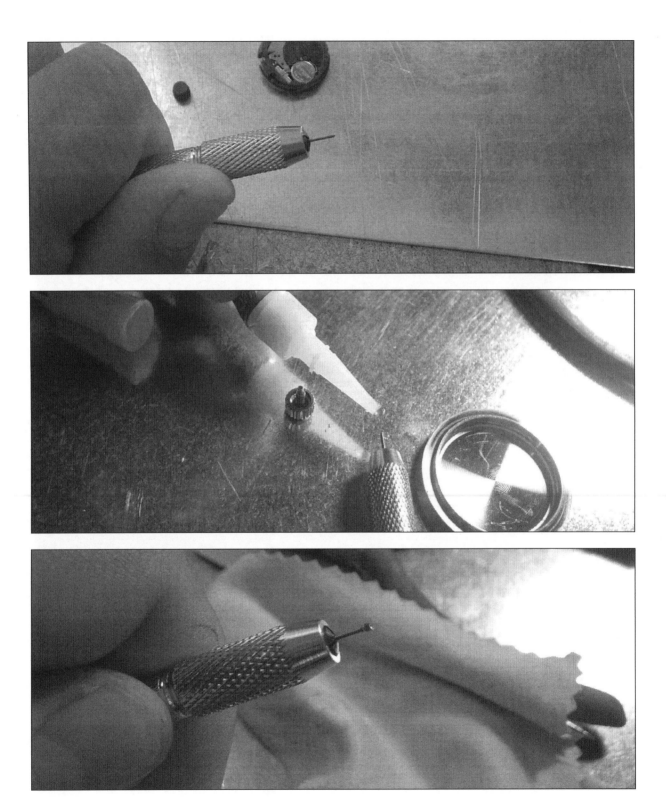

Here is the short stem with the long stem extender glued on. Next you are going to screw on the crown and insert the stem back into the movement to check the length. Determine how much of the stem extender needs to be cut off for the crown to fit snugly against the side of the case. Now, remove the stem and crown from the movement. Cut off the excess stem a little bit at a time. This takes some trial and error, so take your time. If you cut off too much of the stem extender, then you will have to start the whole project over.

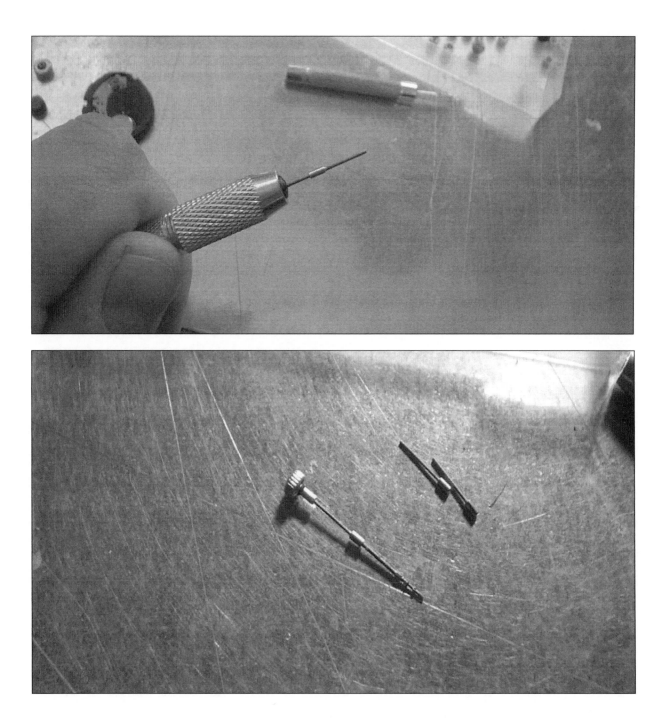

Cut off the excess stem. Add glue, and screw on the crown around 5 or 6 turns before the glue dries. It's ok if the crown doesn't screw on super tight, since the glue will lock the crown in place. *Note: You can always remove the crown once the glued has dried with the help of some pliers and a pin vise.*

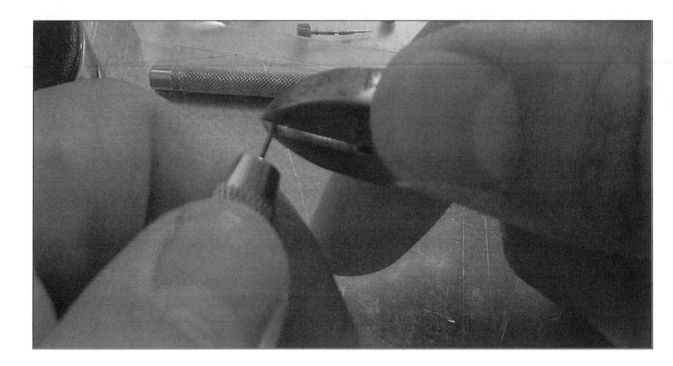

The stem and crown are now ready for installation.

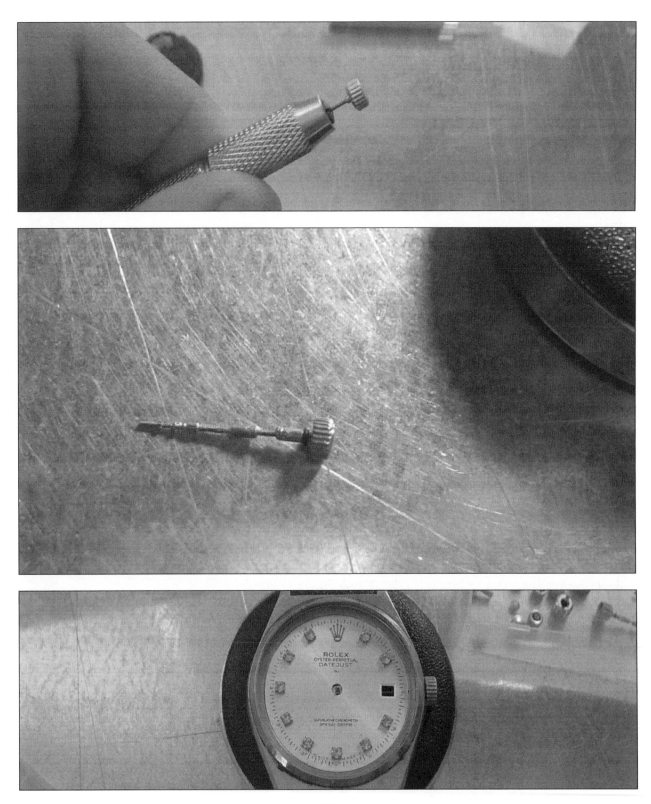

The stem extender kits will also allow you to use a different size stem for the movement, and a different size stem extender for the crown. So you can build a diving watch with a small stem (tap 13, .60 mm) and a large stem extender (tap 9, 1mm). This will allow you to use a small quartz movement inside a big diving watch with a larger crown (tap 9, 1mm) .

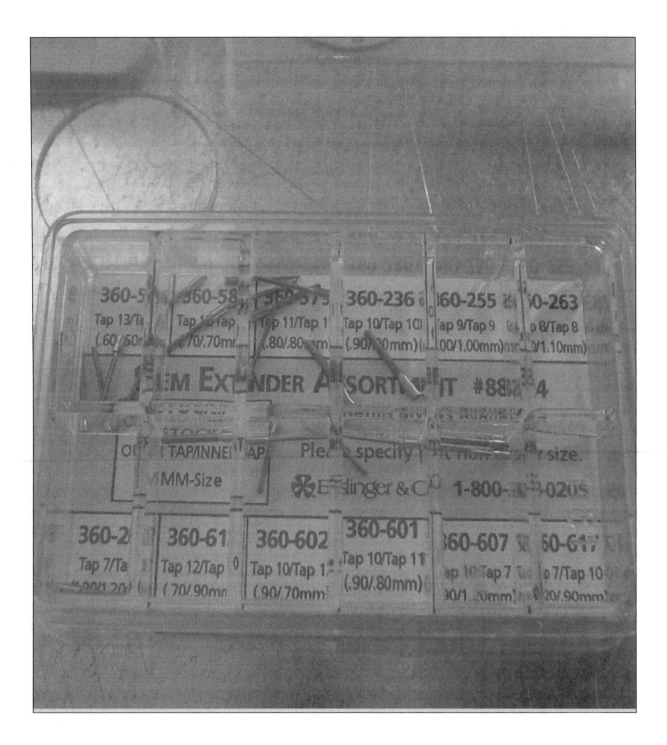

Measure the threaded portion of the stem to determine the tap size. The tap size of the stem extender being measured below is 9 (1 mm).

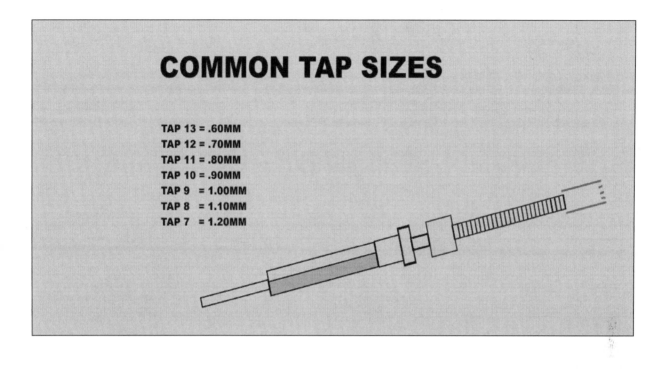

COMMON TAP SIZES

TAP 13 = .60MM
TAP 12 = .70MM
TAP 11 = .80MM
TAP 10 = .90MM
TAP 9 = 1.00MM
TAP 8 = 1.10MM
TAP 7 = 1.20MM

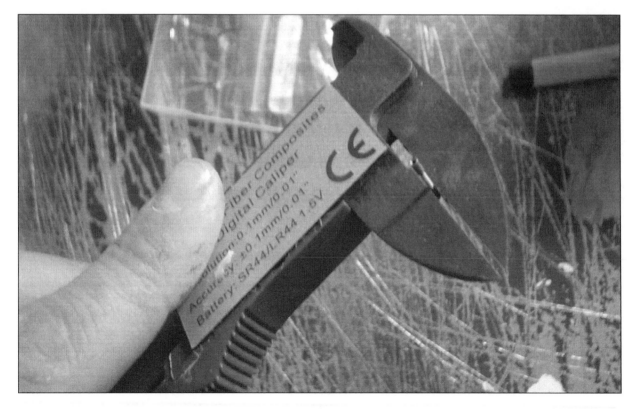

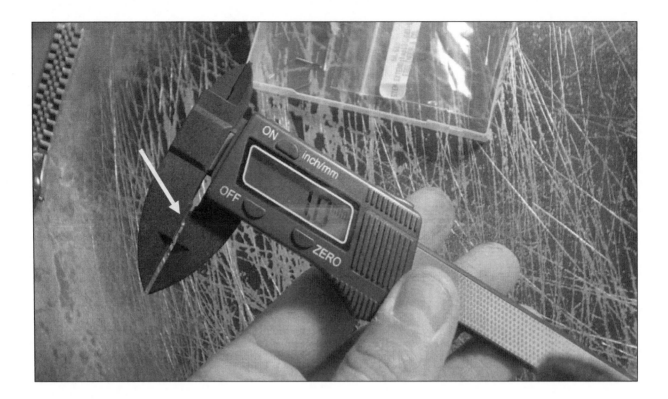

ISOPROPYL ALCOHOL   (OPTIONAL)

This stuff comes in handy if you need to remove the graphics from your watch dial. Be careful though, you can remove all of the dial paint if you use it too long. A q-tip and some alcohol works on most dials with ink printing.

This Seiko dial would be perfect if some of the black dial paint didn't get wiped away as well.

MOVEMENT HOLDER   (OPTIONAL)

Here is a sliding plastic movement or case holder. It comes in handy when you have to work on the backside of the movement after the watch hands are in place. It holds the movement by putting pressure on the sides of the dial. You can find them on Ebay by looking under the search term "plastic watch case holder." They cost around $9.

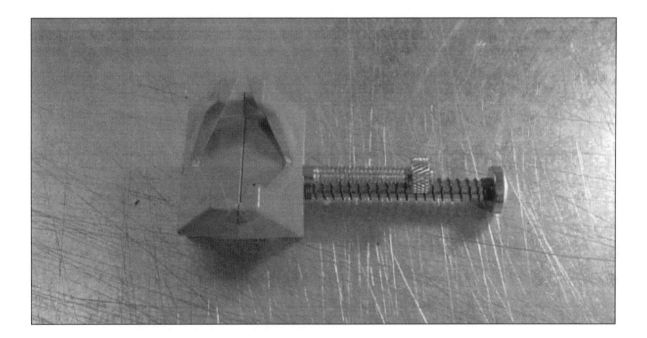

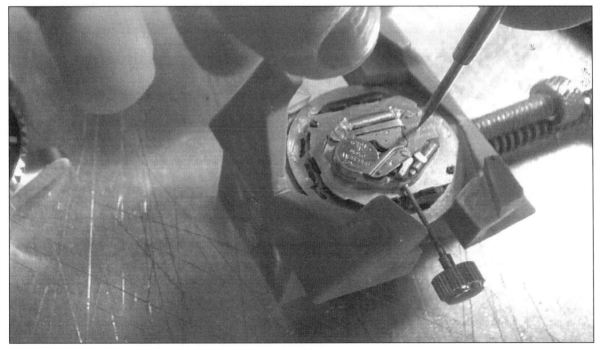

MINI CLIPS   (OPTIONAL)

These are very small chip clips that can hold the dial and movement in place if you need to use glue when a movement holder is not available. This process will be explained in detail later on in the book. These mini clips are available at your local hardware store.

LUMINOUS PAINT   (OPTIONAL)

If you have an old set of watch hands that need to be re-lumed, you can paint them with several new coats of luminous paint. This process takes a bunch of practice and a good brush, so I wouldn't recommend it unless you are really into restoring old watch parts. New watch hands are just too inexpensive these days. Type in "luminous watch paint" on Ebay, or check out http://www.noctilumina.com for info about Noctilumina, which can stay lit for 24 hours in the dark.

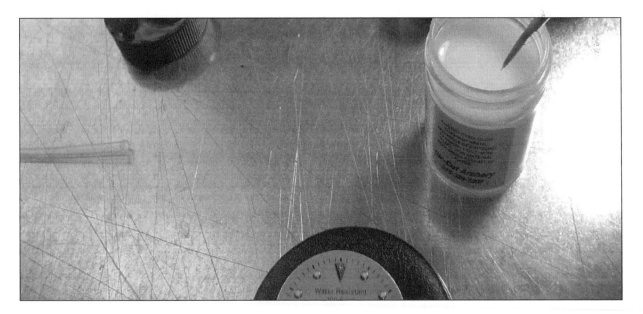

To get a good lume job, you have to paint on several layers of luminous paint. Be sure to remove the old lume with a toothpick before painting.

You can paint the hands, too. Use a toothpick to hold the hand while painting. Don't forget to remove the old lume with a toothpick.

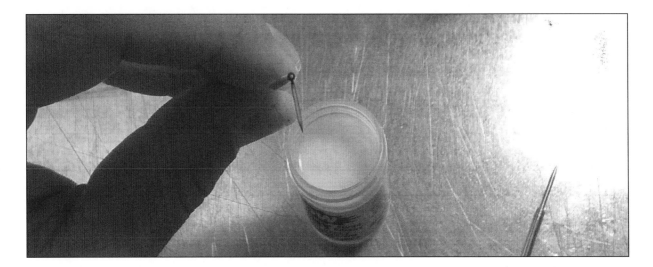

MEASURING YOUR WATCH

When building watches, measurements can be your best friend or your worst enemy. When everything "fits" and is the correct size, you will find that watch building is often quick and easy. But when the parts you are using are from different manufacturers and are different sizes, watch building can at times be quite frustrating. However, this is where the challenge lies for many builders. You might have to adapt to the situation and come up with a new solution that is not written about in any book. If you can do this, then you will be able to build great watches for next to nothing. Hopefully when you are done reading this book, you will be able to go on Ebay and search for a "watch lot", buy a lot of used watches for $10-$20, and then build a custom watch using new and old parts.

Before we get to that point, let's talk about the vital measurements that you must know when buying watch parts. Notice the diagram below for a Quemex watch case. Everything fits perfectly. The dial is 28.8mm in diameter. The space available for the dial is 29mm wide. So any dial 29mm or smaller will fit in this particular watch case. The chapter ring is 27.5mm in diameter. The available space for a chapter ring is 27.8mm, so it will fit just fine, too. Note: Seiko dive watches often have the chapter ring installed by removing the crystal first. In this example, the chapter ring goes in just like the movement, by opening the case back.

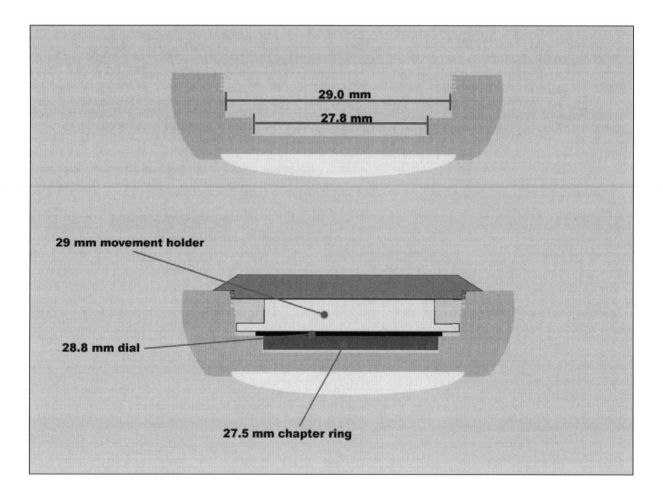

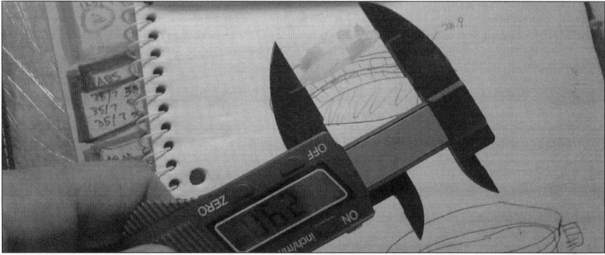

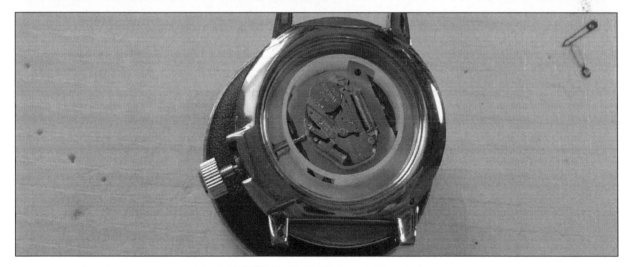

The movement holder is 29mm in diameter. It fits snugly inside the case. The space available for the holder is 29mm. This perfect fit means that the holder will hold everything in place. The dial won't move at all when the watch is worn. If the movement holder is smaller than 29mm, then it is possible the movement and dial will shift left and right every time you pull out the crown to adjust the time. Too much movement in the dial and movement can cause the watch hands to touch the case or crystal and fall off, or worse yet, cause the stem or movement to be damaged. The stem is very easy to break if lateral forces are placed on it. So if the movement shifts inside the case, the stem will be at an angle and can break when you push in the crown.

If the movement holder is not snug, or if you don't have a movement holder (some odd shaped movements do not have holders readily available), then you can apply a small amount glue to the dial and movement. That is, of course, if your dial fits snugly. You still need a 29mm dial if this is the case. A loose dial or movement just won't work. In other words, the dial or the movement holder has to absorb the forces generated by wearing a watch. The dial or holder also has to stop any unwanted movement inside the watch case. If there is nothing preventing the movement from shifting inside the case, then all of the force will be placed on the stem, which will eventually break.

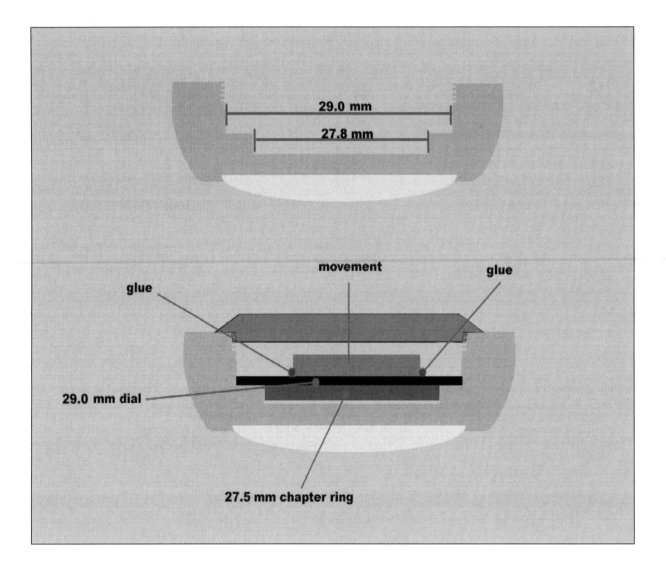

You have to be extremely careful when applying small amounts of glue to a watch dial and movement. If you are not careful, the glue could run and get in between the dial and the movement, causing gears to freeze up. So make sure to use a gel type of crazy glue that does not run. The glue needs to touch the side of the movement and the backside of the dial. Three or four small drops is all that's needed to hold the movement firmly in place. Keep the glue away from any important parts on the movement. *Note: This type of quick fix works best with lightweight quartz movements. If you are using a mechanical movement, always purchase or fabricate a real movement holder.*

In the example below, the movement holder fit the movement, but was too small for the case, so it was glued to the dial instead of the movement. This prevented glue from ending up on any moving parts.

You can use the mini clips to hold the dial and movement in place when applying the glue.

When using glue, you have to pay very close attention to the stem angle. This is essential for determining the correct position of the movement. Normally, the stem comes out of the three o'clock position on most watches, so it is pretty easy to line up. But when the stem comes out at a different angle, you have to be sure to get it right before applying the glue. If the stem is out of line with the movement, it could snap. Notice the watch below. It looks like the stem should come out at the four o'clock position on the dial. But it actually comes out of the case above the four o'clock position.

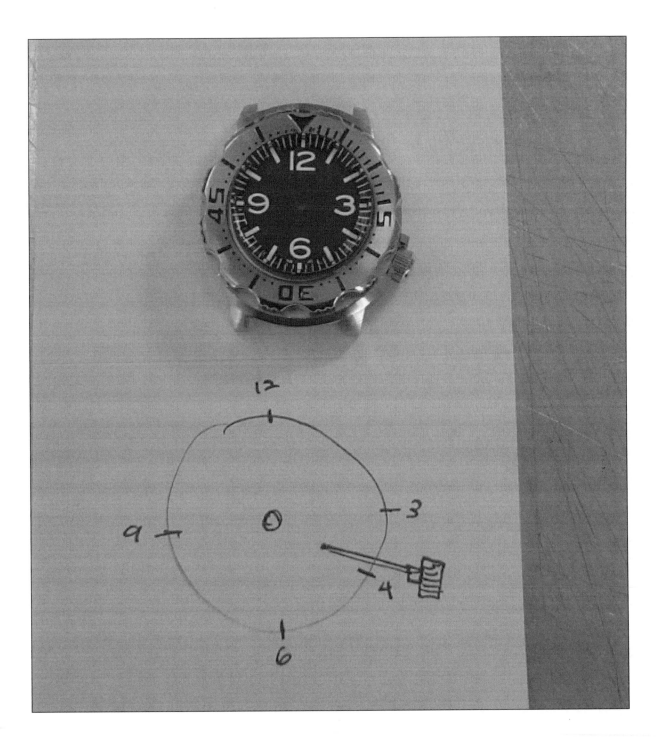

There are a few more parts that you will need to know the measurements of. The hand size, stem and crown size, and the case size.

1. Hand Size

The hand size is determined by the movement. When you purchase a movement, it will tell you the hand sizes that fit on the movement pinions.

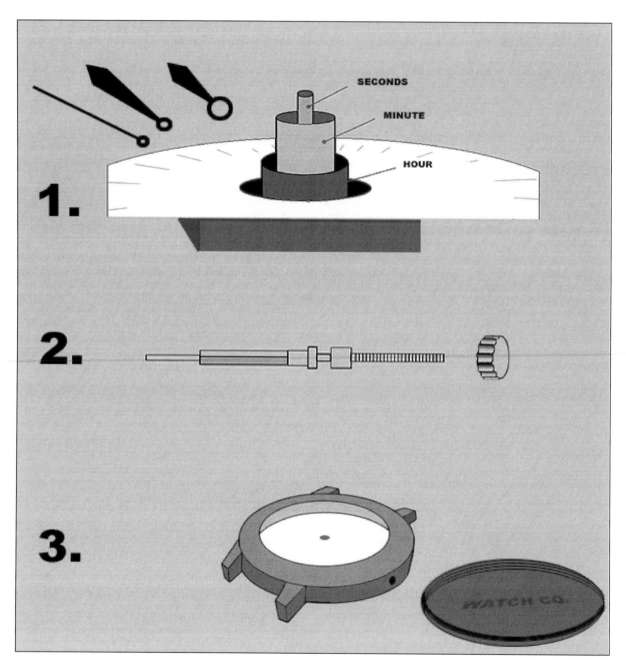

If you look at the Otto Frei website, you can get a better understanding of what I mean. The image below is from the ETA/ESA quartz movement webpage (http://www.ofrei.com/page550.html). The movement below (ESA 805.111) cost $12. It uses three hands: hour=1.20mm, minute=0.70mm, second=0.20mm. The movement size is 11.5 Lignes. If you want to use a dial with a date hole, it must be located at the three o'clock position. The stem also comes out of the three o'clock position. It is made in Switzerland.

ESA 805.111-SWISS
$12.50
ESA 805.111-SWISS

Ligne Size 11.5, height 3.4 , functions: Date at 3, uses 3 hands 70/120/20, Swiss made.

2. Crown and Stem Size

The stem and crown need to have the same tap sizes so the crown can screw on to the stem post. If you need to switch the movement in your watch, the tap size might change, which would require a different stem, or stem extender with a different tap size on each end. It's always a good idea to have extra crowns available, either from the Esslinger website or from watch part lots on Ebay.

3. The case

If you are searching for a case for your watch project, make sure the case back and crystal are in good condition so they do not have to be replaced. If you replace the crystal and do a bad job at it, the watch will not be water resistant. Some brands like Seiko often use the same size watch parts in many of their models. So if you purchased a used $10 Seiko case without a case back, it would be very easy to find another Seiko case back that would fit perfectly. This is why Seiko's are a favorite watch for builders who like to modify their watches, because spare Seiko parts fit Seiko cases. Last but not least, you will also need to know the lug width if you plan on changing the watch band.

BUILDING YOUR WATCH

Before you begin building your dream watch, it's a good idea to get some practice in. You want to get proficient in removing the watch movement, removing the stem, unscrewing the crown, screwing the crown back on, taking off the hands, putting them back on, and installing the movement back in the case. One way to get experience is by practicing on inexpensive watches before start working on more expensive types. You can find watches on Ebay made by Philip Persio or Schaffer for dirt cheap, often having a retail price of $16 or less. Also check under the search terms "submariner watch" and "military watch". Pictured below is a Schaffer automatic submariner that I got on Ebay for $20.

Now let's get started with a very basic watch build. I will be taking a complete watch head (which is an assembled watch minus the band) and changing the hands for a different look. This project will also show you how to replace the movement with a similar movement, or replace the dial with a similar dial.

Below you can see all of the parts needed for this build. The 18mm rubber band with orange stitching is from Ebay. If you search under the term "black rubber band orange" you can find them for as low as $10. The watch head is from the Otto Frei website (http://www.ofrei.com/page1039.html). If you look on that page you will see item number WH-84. The water resistant case is made from stainless steel and has a screw down crown and case back. It comes with a quartz ESA 805.121 movement, which is 11.5 Lignes. The specs for the movement are located on this page, http://www.ofrei.com/page550.html. The hand sizes are 70/120/20, which means that the hour hand is 1.20mm, the minute hand is 0.70mm, and the second hand is 0.20mm. The dial is 28.5mm wide, with a minute track diameter of 26mm. That means this dial is designed for hands that are 13mm or smaller in length. Anything longer than 13mm will extend out past the second indicators and will probably touch the case. The minute markings, and probably get stuck against the case wall. So a 12mm or 11mm maximum hand length should work just fine for this watch.

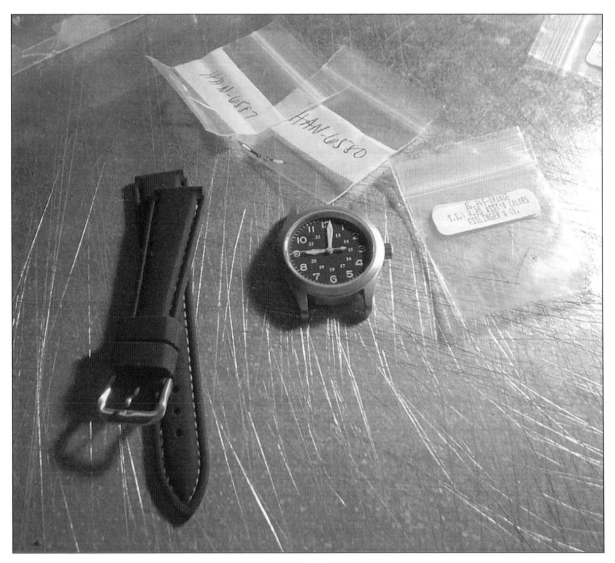

Since I will be changing the hands on this watch, I ordered some 70/120 hands from this page, http://www.ofrei.com/page577.html. The item numbers are HAN-6580 and HAN-6587. I ordered two sets because I wanted a different color for each hand ($4 per set). The white hour hand is 7.5mm long and the minute hand is 11.5mm long. The 0.20mm orange luminous sweep second hand is from the Esslinger website, http://www.esslinger.com/hole20sweepsecondhands-assortedcolors.aspx. It is always a good idea to buy extra seconds hands, since they are very easy to damage. These hands come in a variety of colors and cost $2 each. The 18mm spring bars for the watch band can be found on the Esslinger, Otto Frei, and Ebay websites. You might want to get a kit with several different sizes if you plan on building many watches. You can order 10 packs in one size for $2.50 from http://www.esslinger.com/refills-stainlesssteeldfsoldinpkgof10.aspx.

Now, let's get started with a basic watch build.

STEP 1 : REMOVE THE BAND

If you purchased a complete watch for your project, then use your spring bar tool and remove the spring bars from the watch case by compressing them.

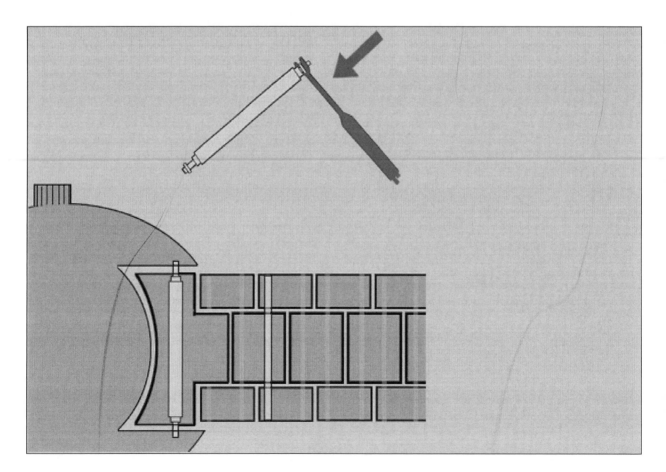

STEP 2 : UNSCREW THE CASE BACK

Remove the case back. Be sure to have the proper case back opener for the watch you purchased. Some case back openers will be able to open both screw-on and Rolex style case backs. The case below was opened with the screw-on style of case opener. I like to put the case in a vise to hold it in place before unscrewing the case back. This will make the job much easier and help prevent slippage and scratches to the case. Be sure to tape up the vise so you do not scratch the lugs. Don't over tighten the vise, you could bend the lugs.

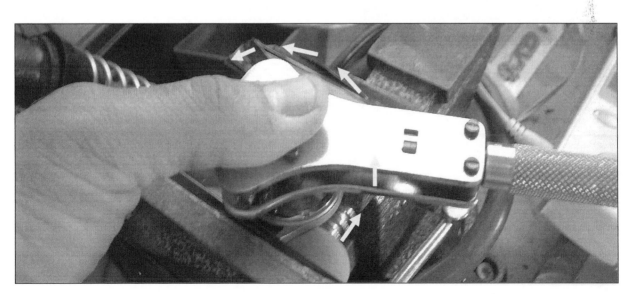

STEP 3 : PULL OUT THE STEM

Find the detent button, or the set lever screw. Push in the button to release the stem, or unscrew the set lever screw a little bit at a time until you can pull out the stem. Sometimes it helps to unscrew the set lever screw a quarter turn, then push in and pull out the stem. If it doesn't work, repeat the process again. If you unscrew the set lever screw too much, the mechanism will become disassembled. **Do not loosen the set lever screw too much.**

The set lever screw was unscrewed and the stem came out. Now use a dental pick or toothpick and remove the plastic movement holder.

STEP 4 : REMOVE THE MOVEMENT HOLDER

Use your dental pick or toothpick and lift up the movement holder. Note: If you have a mechanical movement and the movement holder is stuck on the movement, you can try lifting the whole movement out a little bit before lifting off the case in step 5.

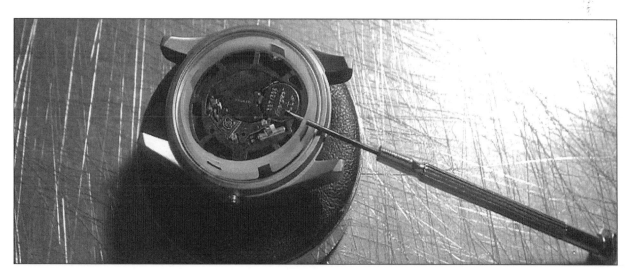

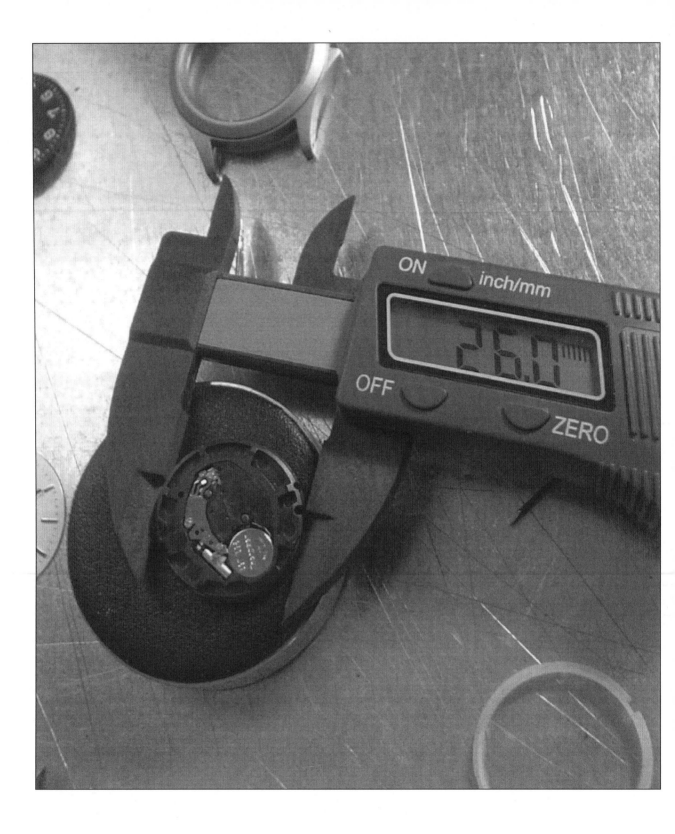

STEP 5 : FLIP THE WATCH OVER

You now need to look at the watch in the face up position, so the case and movement need to do a flip. After you have removed the movement holder, take your movement pad out from underneath the watch and place it over the movement, so that the leather is touching backside of the movement. Now flip over the movement pad and watch.

STEP 6 : LIFT THE CASE OFF OF THE MOVEMENT

Grab the case and lift it off the movement.

Here is a mechanical automatic watch. The movement holder is pulled up out of the case just enough to free up the movement. Now you can flip over the watch, and the movement will come out.

STEP 7 : REMOVE THE HANDS

Use your toothpick and line the hands up. Now place a dial protector underneath the hands.

Use your hand remover to lift the hands off of the movement pinions.

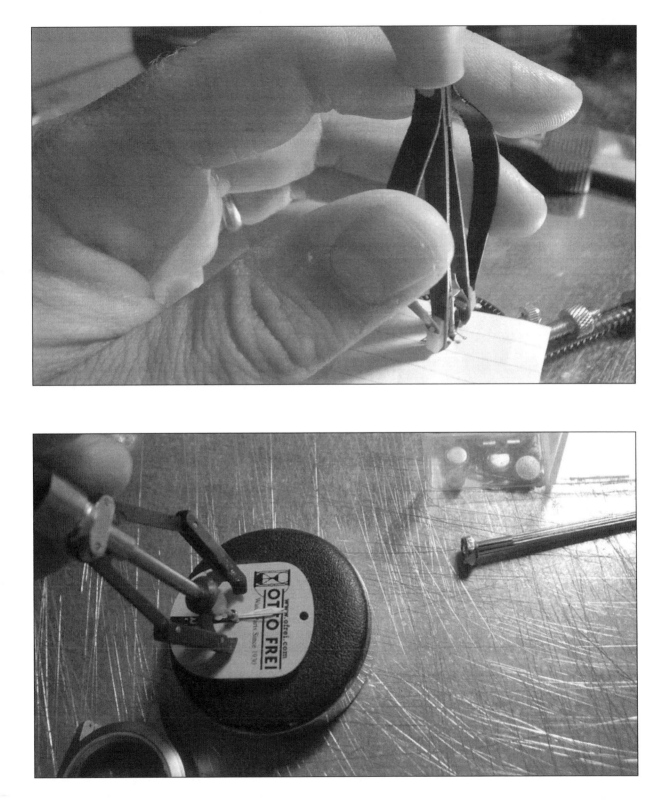

Line up the hands and lift them off of the pinions and hour wheel. The hand remover's hooks will be underneath all three hands, so when you compress its springs, the hand remover will lift the hands upward and off of the watch movement.

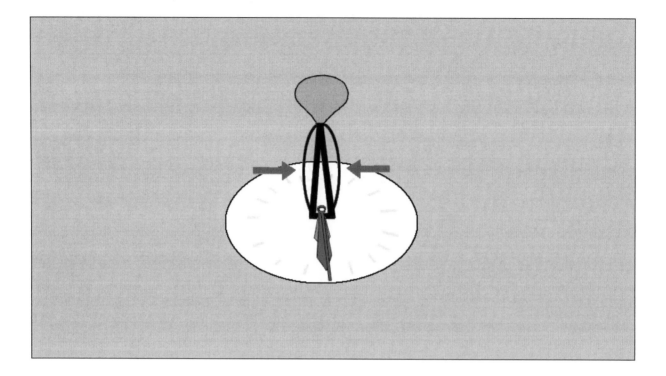

STEP 8 : CHANGE THE DIAL

Now is the time to change the dial if you want. If you look at the sides of the movement, you will see two small metal dial feet that stick into the movement. These keep the dial in the proper position at all times. You can pry off the dial with a metal pick or small screwdriver. Be careful not to touch any gears.

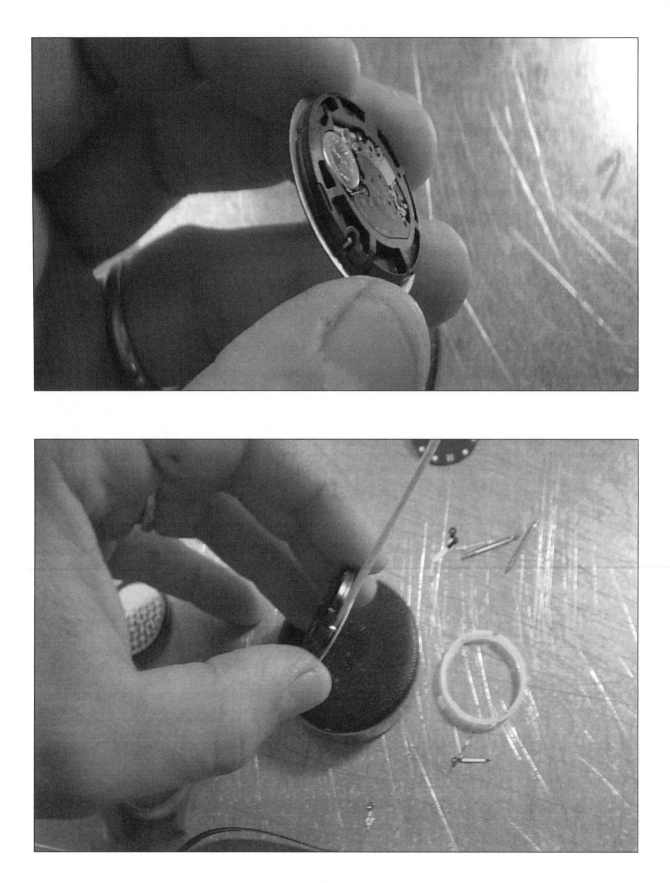

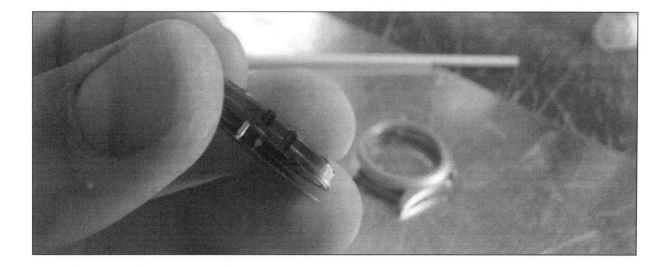

Note: make sure that the dial is positioned properly in the case. The perimeter of the dial should touch the case. If there are any unwanted gaps, check the position of the movement holder and movement.

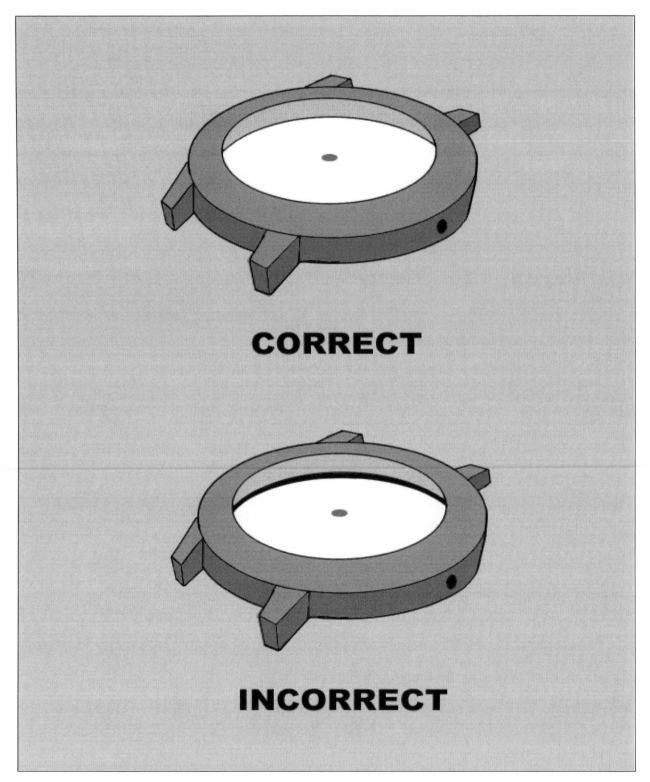

CORRECT

INCORRECT

WHAT IF YOU HAVE A MECHANICAL WATCH MOVEMENT?

If your movement is a mechanical one, then the dial feet will normally be positioned along the outside of the movement perimeter. In many cases, the dial feet will be held in position by a small screw. Loosen the screws, and the dial can be removed.

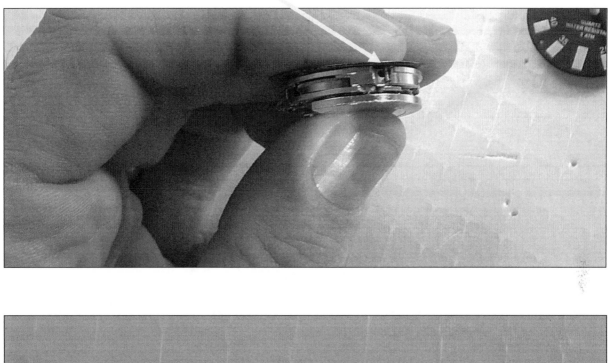

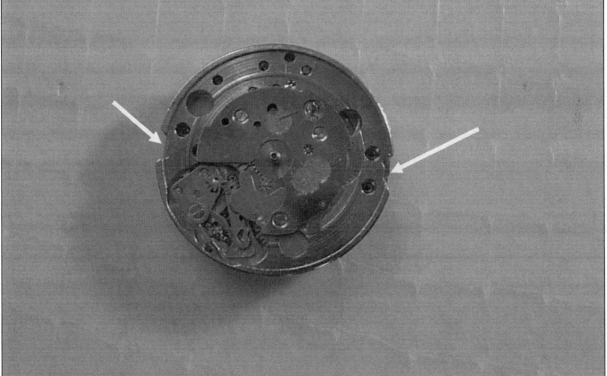

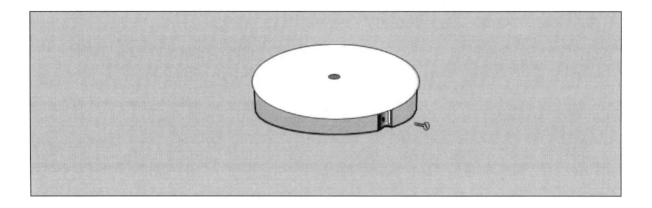

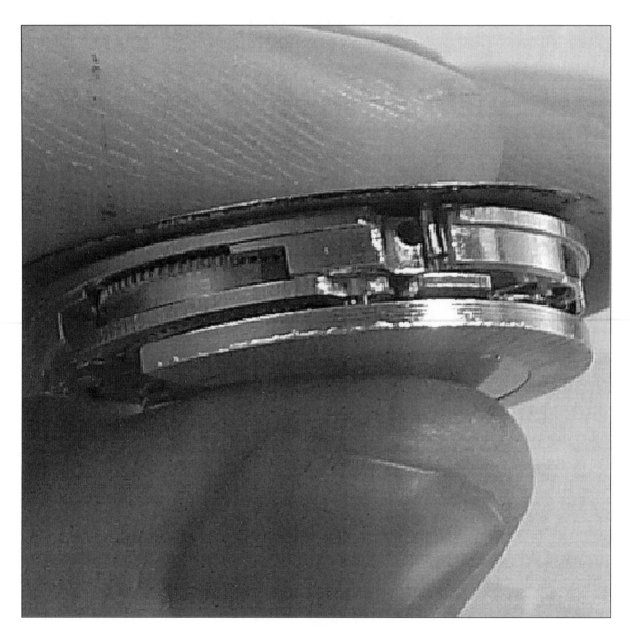

Now you can put the new dial on your watch. If the new dial is by the same brand, and the dial feet match up, then you can simply place the dial feet in the existing movement holes.

OPTION 1: There are many methods that you can use to add a dial to a movement that it is not designed for. Each method requires some skill and plenty of practice. You will probably get really good at one of these methods over time. The only problem is figuring out which method you like the best. First, let's try to replace the dial feet on the new dial. To do this, we need to remove the dial feet on the new dial with wire cutters, a dremel tool, or a file.

The dial on the left is the new one. Its feet are now off. The dial on the right is the one we are replacing. Place a toothpick through the old dial's center hole, and press the dial into a sheet of paper that is placed on top of a Styrofoam board. Mark down the 12, 3, 6, and 9 positions on the paper. Note: Large sheets of the Styrofoam pictured below actually blew into my yard from a construction site. That happens a lot when you move into a new neighborhood. I imagine you can find this stuff at any of the big hardware stores. It seems to work great.

The markings from the old dial feet are now present on the sheet of paper.   Use a small clip and a toothpick to attach the new dial to the paper.

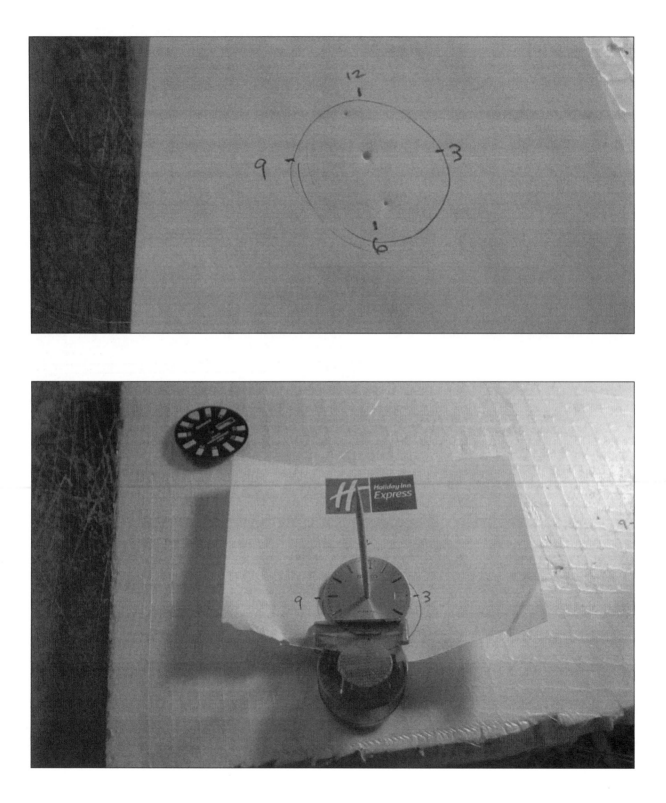

Now use a marker to mark the holes on the back of the dial. Push the marker head through the holes in the paper.

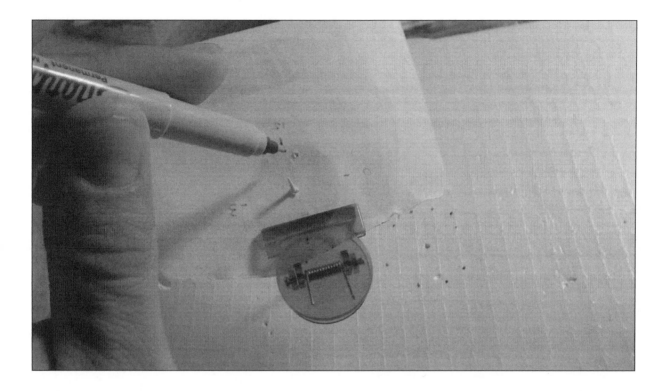

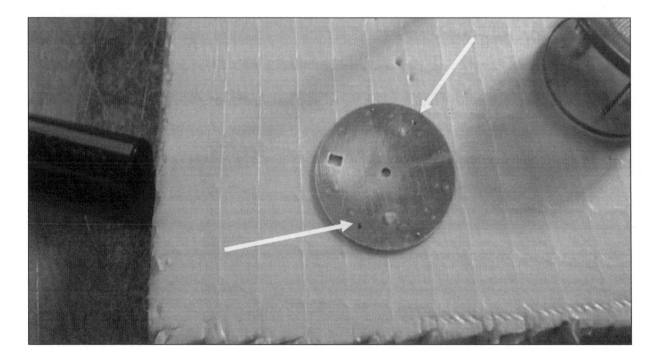

Now we are going to use some vintage style 22 AWG wire from http://stores.ebay.com/Classic-Clones-Amplification to make the new dial feet. It's light and stiff, so perfect for the job. I love using this wire because there are literally tons of uses for this stuff. We will also need some type of super strong glue. This is really the key to the success or failure of this job. A high quality glue is essential to make this work. After the new dial feet have been glued on, don't touch the dial until the glue has completely dried.

The glue has been added to the marker ink spots on the back of the dial. Now cut the 22 AWG wire, remove the braid cloth, and touch it to the glue drops. Stick the other end of the wire in the Styrofoam board to give it some support. Remove the dial when the glue has dried.

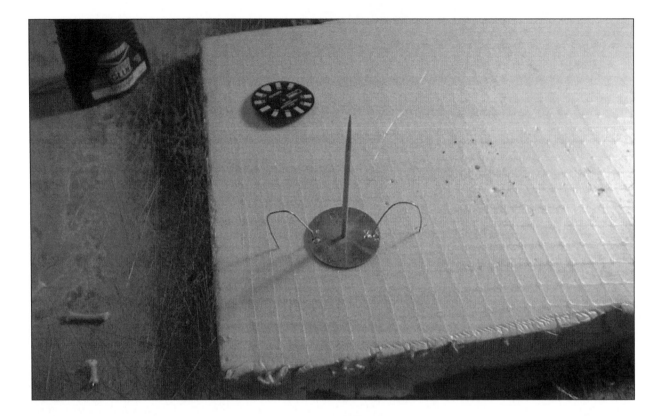

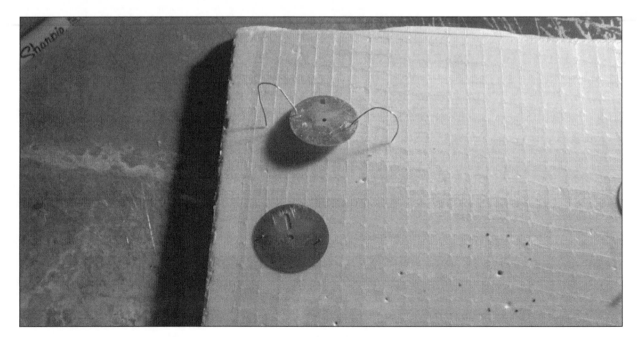

Now cut the dial feet down to size. Add more glue if needed. If you need to straighten out the newly made dial feet, you can place the dial back into the Styrofoam holes. Use a dremel tool if you need to remove some of the excess glue. This technique requires practice and some good glue.

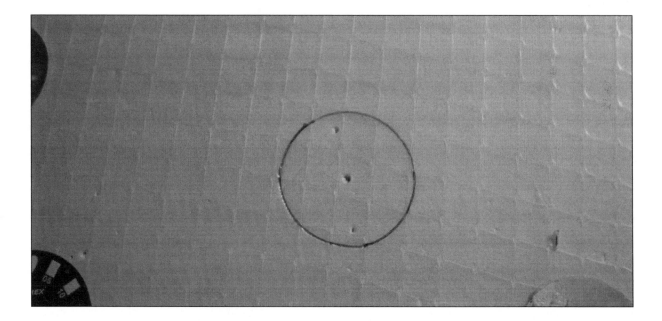

OPTION 2: If the plastic movement holder fits snugly inside the case, then you might be able to add dial dots, or small double sided tape to the movement to hold the dial in place after the dial feet have been removed.

After you have cut off the dial feet, use your tweezers to lift the dial dots from the sheet. Then place the dots on the movement face. Make sure not to place them over any moving parts or gears. Now lift off the non-sticky piece of brown paper. Now line up the dial correctly and press it on the movement. The dial should hold in place until the movement goes into the case, but it still can be shifted a little bit if needed. Once the movement is in the case, the movement holder will apply enough pressure to keep everything in place.

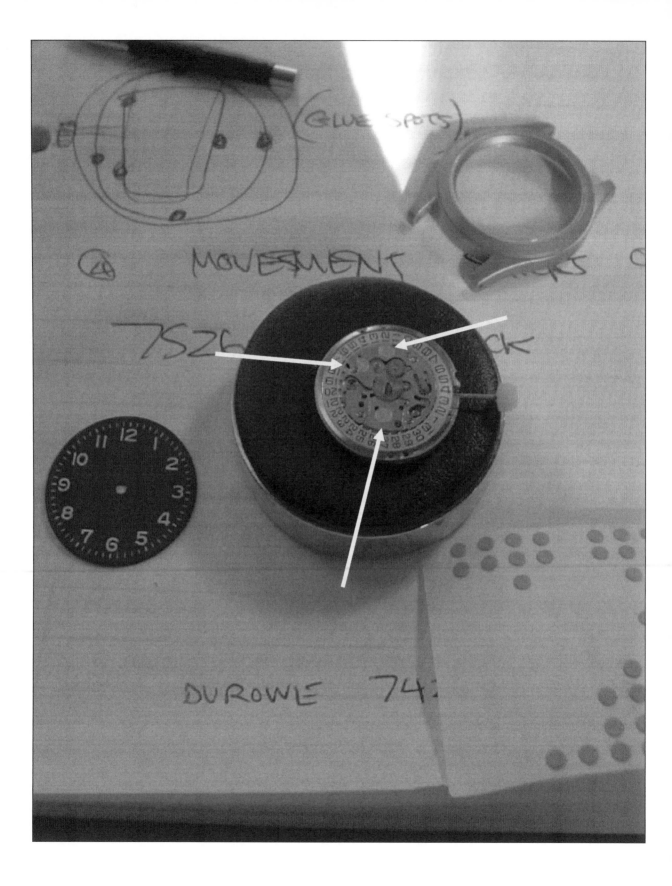

Press the dial into the dial dots, and finish building the watch.

Note: The movement pictured below has a day and date wheel so it won't work with the dial feet. There is nowhere to place them.

WHAT IF I DONT HAVE A MOVEMENT HOLDER?

OPTION 1: If you don't have a movement holder, the easiest solution would be to buy an assortment of movement holders for the movement size you are using from www.ofrei.com. The movement holders can be cut with scissors or filed down around the edges to get a tight fit inside the case.

OPTION 2: If you can't find a movement holder to fit your movement, you can always fabricate one with Speedi-fit putty, which is described in detail earlier in this book. This technique will take some practice, so try it out on your junk watches first.

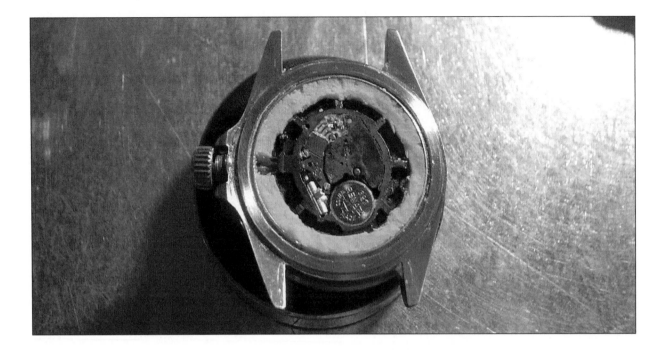

You will need to shave off around the perimeter of the Speedi-fit movment holder, so that there is room for the case back to engage the case threads.

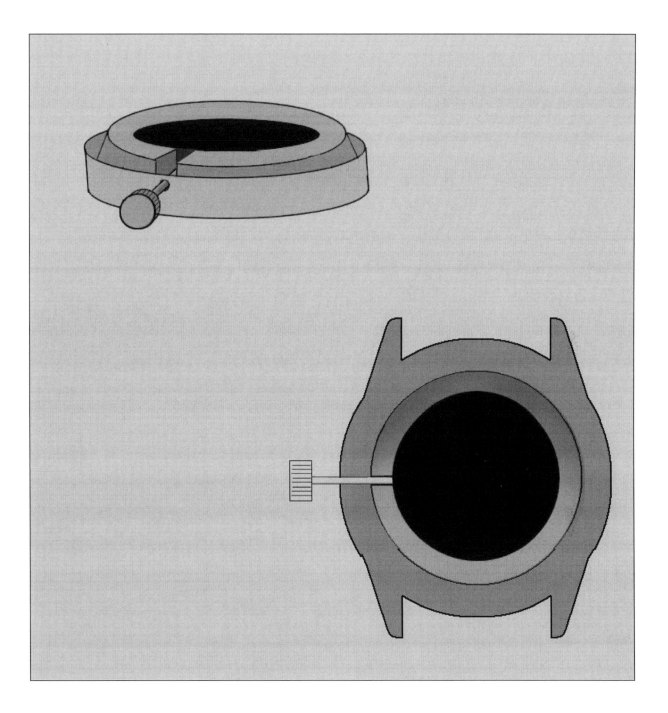

Note: If you put the Speedi-fit in the case first, then press down on the putty with a junk movement and then cut out the movement outline, you will find that the movement will often be positioned improperly. Only when the movement is in place first can you be sure that the Speedi-fit has not altered the stem angle. I would not recommend doing it the way shown below unless you have plenty of experience retro-fitting watch movements.

OPTION 3: There are other ways to build a movement holder. When you think about it, almost any type of substance can be used. Let's take a look at a movement holder made out of cardboard. The watch we are making this holder for has a diameter of 28.5mm for the dial and 28.5mm for the movement holder, so we will make the cardboard holder that size. First, find a stiff piece of cardboard and cut out the center hole for the movement pinions that hold the hands. Then place the movement over the cardboard and trace it out.

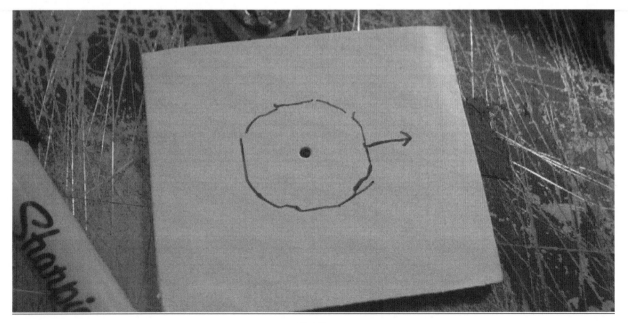

Now draw the 28.5mm circle for the movement holder that fits into the watch case. If your dial is 28.5mm, you can trace it, or measure out the diameter with your calliper. It is 14.25mm from the center to the outside perimeter of the circle.

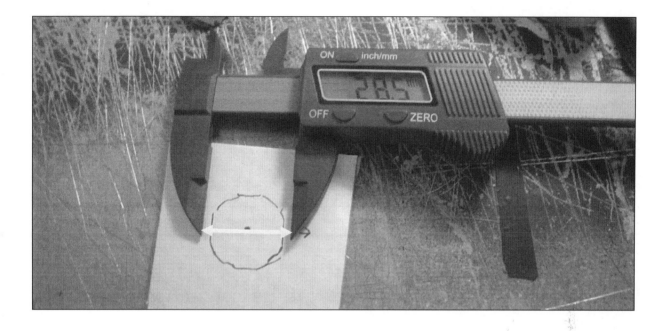

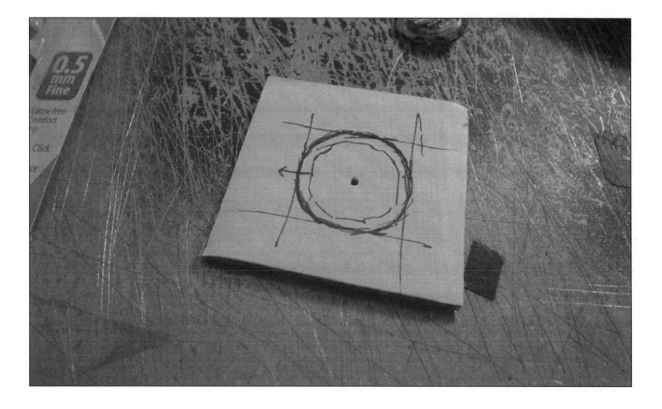

Now cut out the movement holder and place it and the movement inside the case. Press it down with your dental pick tool. Feel free to paint the cardboard with acrylic paint and a thin paintbrush.

Don't like cardboard, how about using shipping tape. Tape 10 pieces of tape together or more, and cut out your movement holder. The nice thing about making a movement holder like this is that it is very cheap to make and mistakes can be quickly corrected. It only takes a few minutes to make one of these holders.

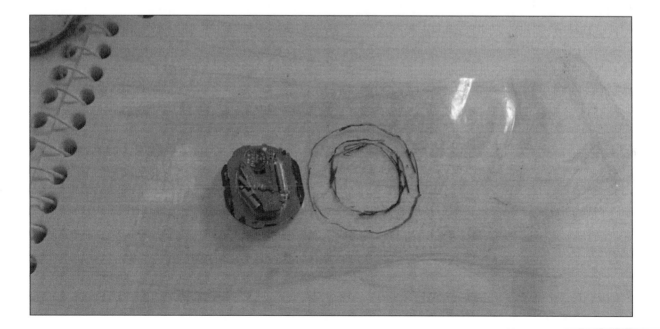

When the tape movement holder is in the case, press it down with the dental pick tool.

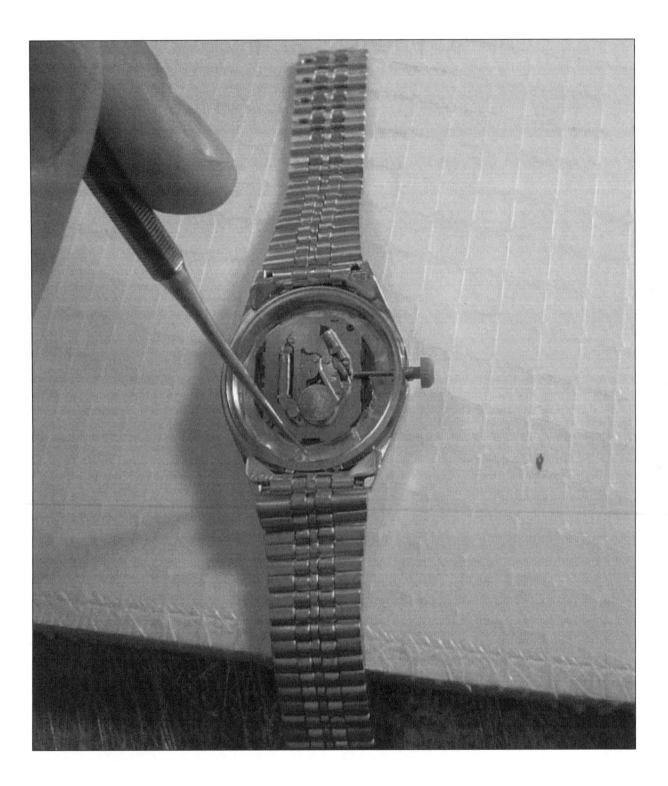

OPTION 4: When nothing else seems to work, you can always use a gel glue to glue the dial to the movement, which is explained earlier in this book. You have to be very careful when using this method. The last thing you want to do is get glue on one of the watch gears or date wheel.

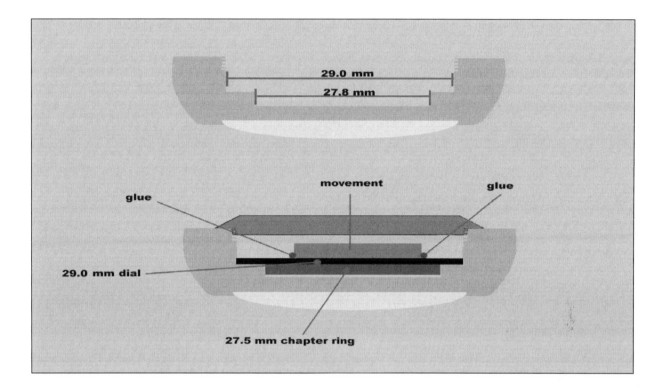

First, use some small clips to line up the dial in the correct position. The seconds pinion should be in the center of the dial hole, and the three o'clock marker should line up with the stem and crown. Now add glue to the back of the movement, on two to four sides. Use only a small amount.

Remove any unwanted marks on the dial with Rodico. You can do this at any time, just be sure the dial is clean before installing the dial and movement into the case. Clean the crystal with a jewellers polishing cloth. Remove all fingerprints and dust particles.

Check the crystal in the light for smudges or dust.

STEP 9 : INSTALLING THE HANDS

Now that the dial is on, it's time to install the hands. The hour and minute hand will be much easier to install than the seconds hand. It might take you several attempts before you are able to get the seconds hand on its tiny pinion. If your positioning is off, you can smash the seconds hand when you press down with the hand setting tool. Don't press down with too much pressure until you are sure you have the hand securely on the pinion. This is something that can't really be described accurately, you just have to get a feel for it through lots of practise. To install the hands, grab them with the tweezers close to the tip, and press down with the setting tool. **Note: before putting the hands on, it's a good idea to install the stem and pull it out to the setting position, so that none of the pinions are moving while you are installing the hands.**

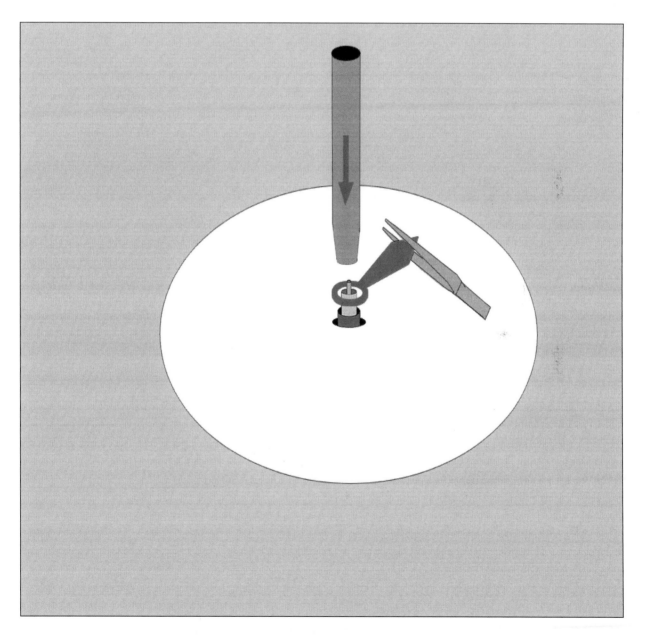

Install the hands in different positions. Don't overlap them. You don't want the tweezers touching the other hands and changing their angle.

After all three hands have been installed, make sure they do not touch one another. Turn the hands by rotating the crown to check for any collisions. If one of the hands is angled too much, it will touch the other hands and stop the watch. So make sure the hands are perfect before installing the movement back inside the case. I have made the mistake of not checking the hands thoroughly before installing the movement, only to have to take the watch apart and reset the hands again.

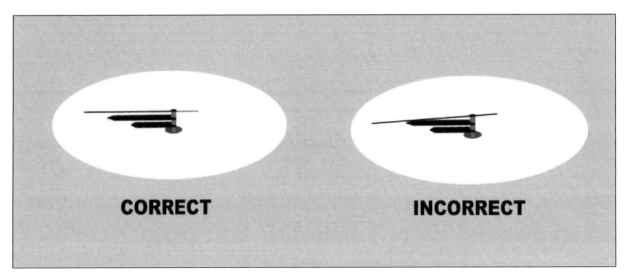

CORRECT   **INCORRECT**

Check the angle of each hand before putting the movement and dial back inside the case.

Now position the hands in the correct position before installing the movement inside the case. Set the hands exactly how you want them to be positioned when the watch advances to a new hour. If you don't do this, when the watch hits two o'clock or three o'clock, the hour hand might not be positioned in front of the correct hour marker. Use a toothpick to move the hour hand or minute hand to the correct position.

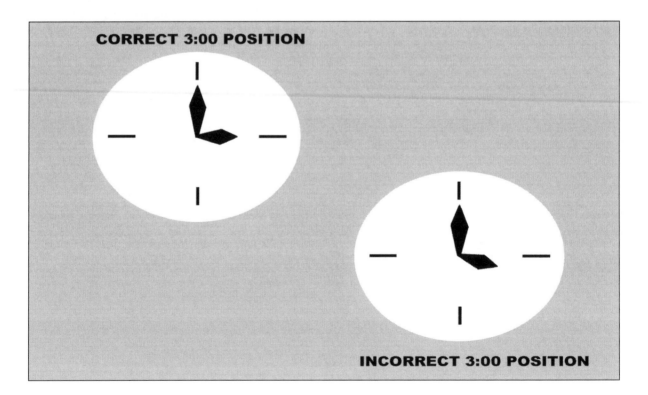

257

When the dial is ready, remove the stem, and then place the watch case over the dial and movement. Make sure to line it up properly so that the three o'clock marker is lined up with the stem. Note: if you can't get the movement and holder to fit inside the case, try placing the case over the movement and dial, then flip it over and install the movement holder.

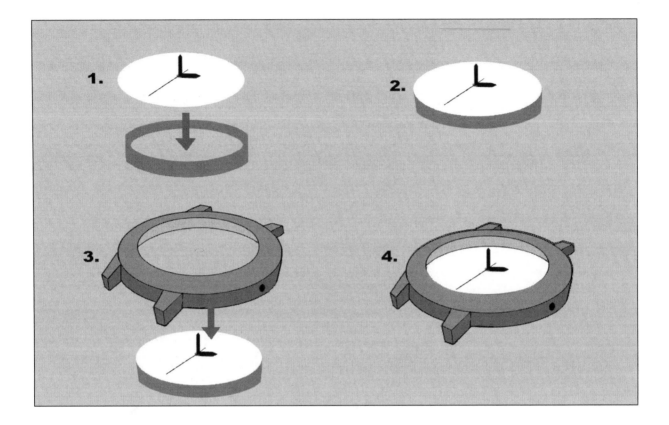

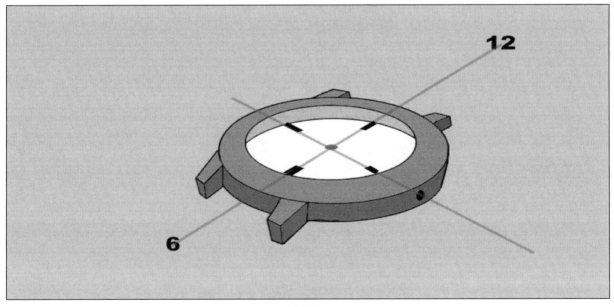

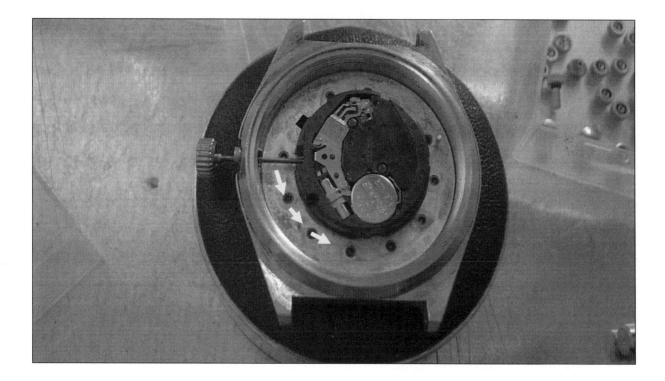

If the dial is off position a little bit after you installed the movement inside the case, you can remove the movement holder, and use a small screwdriver or dental pick to rotate the dial a tiny bit. If you rotate the dial too much, the hands will be off by a few minutes.

The dial is now in position. Flip the movement and case over and install the stem back into the movement. Push in the detent button and push in the stem. Or if you have a set lever screw on your movement, be sure to screw it back down. Otherwise, the stem will fall out of the movement when you try to adjust the time.

STEP 10 : ADDING THE GREASE

The watch now needs a watertight seal. For this task we will use Silcon 7 grease on the case back gasket, and also on the case tube and crown. Make sure to apply grease on the case and crown threads. You can use a toothpick to apply the grease.

STEP 11 : SCREW ON THE CASE BACK AND SCREW DOWN THE CROWN

It's time to screw everything down so that the watch becomes water resistant. I like to hold the case in a vice when I screw down the case back.

Screw the crown down. The watch is now ready for the band.

STEP 12 : INSTALL THE WATCH BAND

Use your spring bar tool to compress the spring bars and install the watch band. The case below needs an 18mm band. You can use your callipers to compress the spring bars you have lying around to check their size. Fully compress them and take a look at the calliper reading.

Use the opposite end of the digital callipers to check the watch lug with. It's around 18mm. Put the spring bar through the hole in the end link. The end of the spring bar should now be inside one of the lug holes. Now use the spring bar tool to compress the spring bar and force the other end into the other case lug hole.

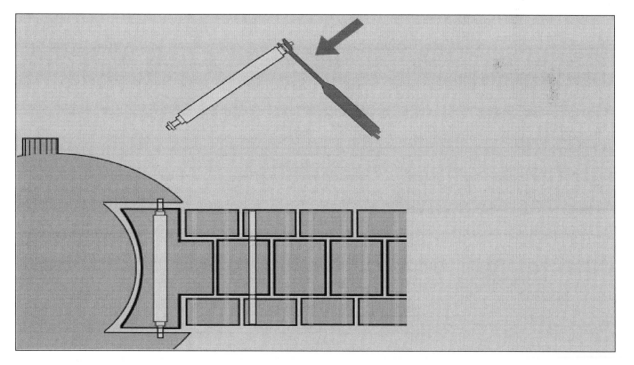

Here is the finished watch.

Here are some other watch projects from beginning to end. Below is a used Seiko SKX007 diver watch that I bought from Ebay for $70. This watch has a great automatic movement (Seiko 7S26) that is reasonably priced, around $45 at www.10watches.com. The new 28.5mm dial that I put on is also from www.10watches.com and it cost around $20. The new 150/90/25 hands are from Ebay.

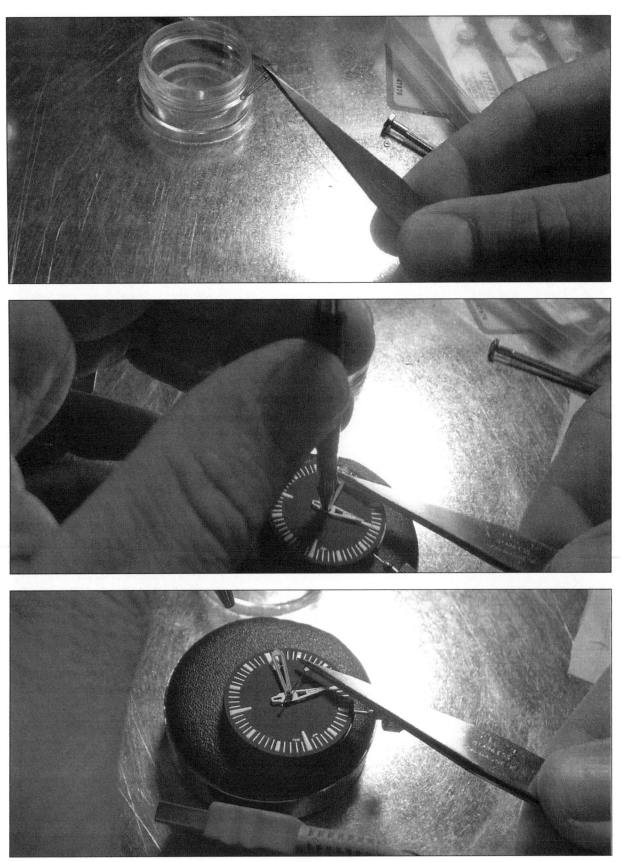

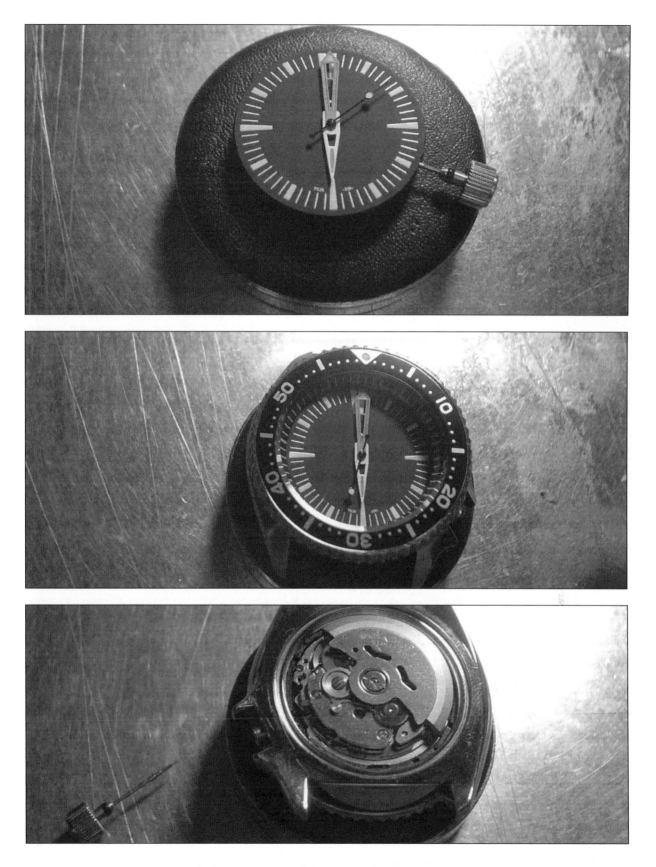

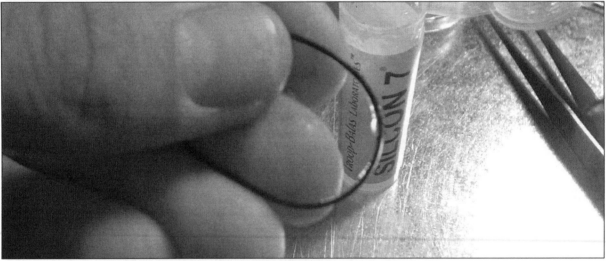

NOTE: YOU NEED TO REGULATE THE TIME BEFORE PUTTING THE CASE BACK ON A MECHANICAL WATCH!!! THIS PROCESS IS DESCRIBED ON PAGE 85.

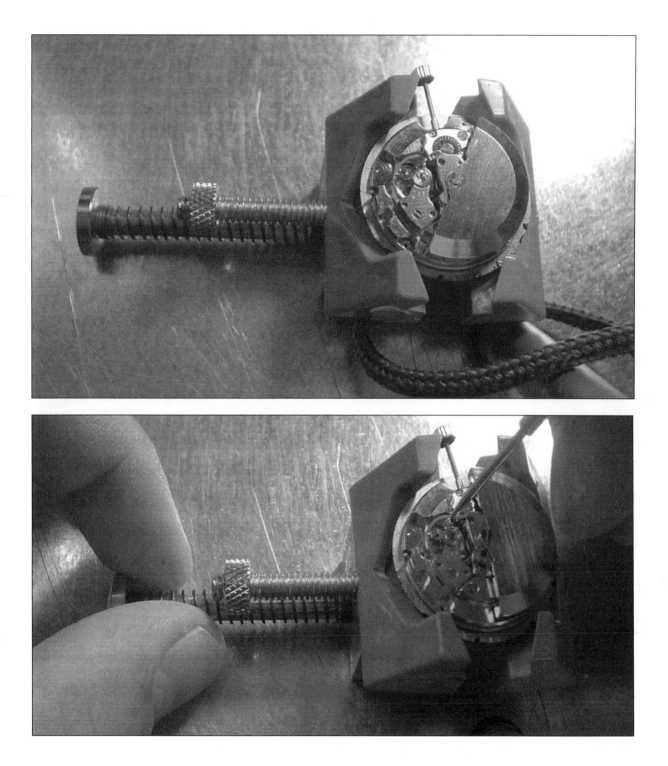

Here is another watch project. Below is a very nice Quemex watch purchased from the website, http://stores.ebay.com/Shop-Hear-First. It comes with a very cool brass case. This watch looks just like the tuna can style of Seiko divers watch. In this project, the dial, band, hands, and movement were replaced. A new Miyota 2115 movement was placed inside the watch. The end result is a pretty cool diving watch at an amazing price.

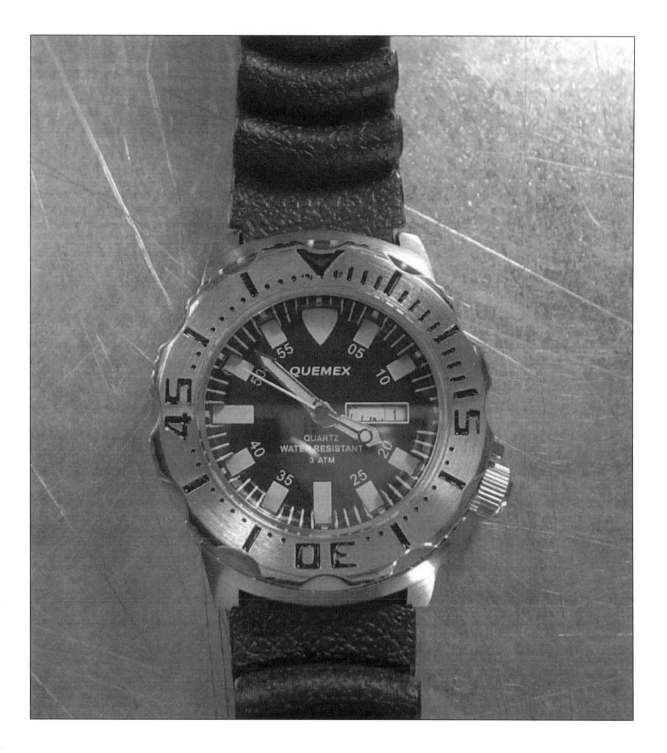

Here is the disassembled stock watch.

Here are the new parts plus the case. The dial is from www.10watches.com. The stock chapter ring was glued on to the new dial face with Hypo Cement. The chapter ring in this watch goes in through the case back, unlike the Seiko divers, where the chapter ring has to be installed through the front of the case after the crystal has been removed. The hands are from www.ofrei.com and use 70/120/17mm hands.

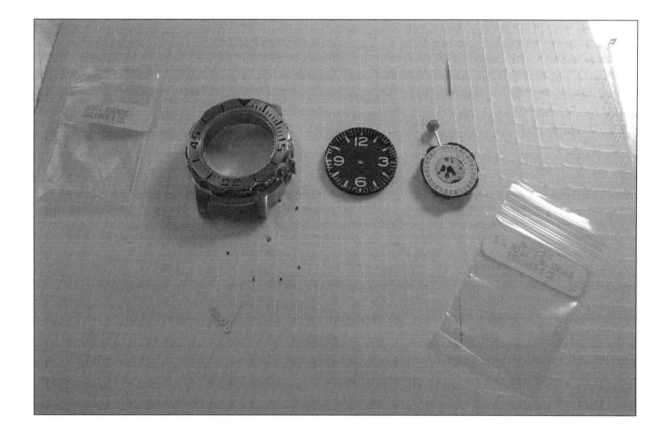

Here is how you glue the chapter ring to the dial. All you need is a tiny bit of glue to hold the ring on to the dial until it gets placed inside the watch case.

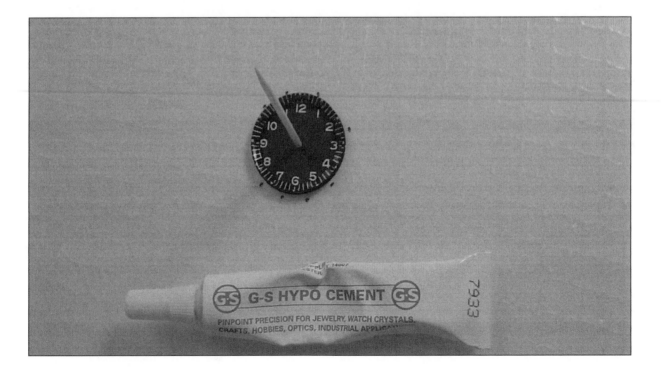

Now put the hands on.

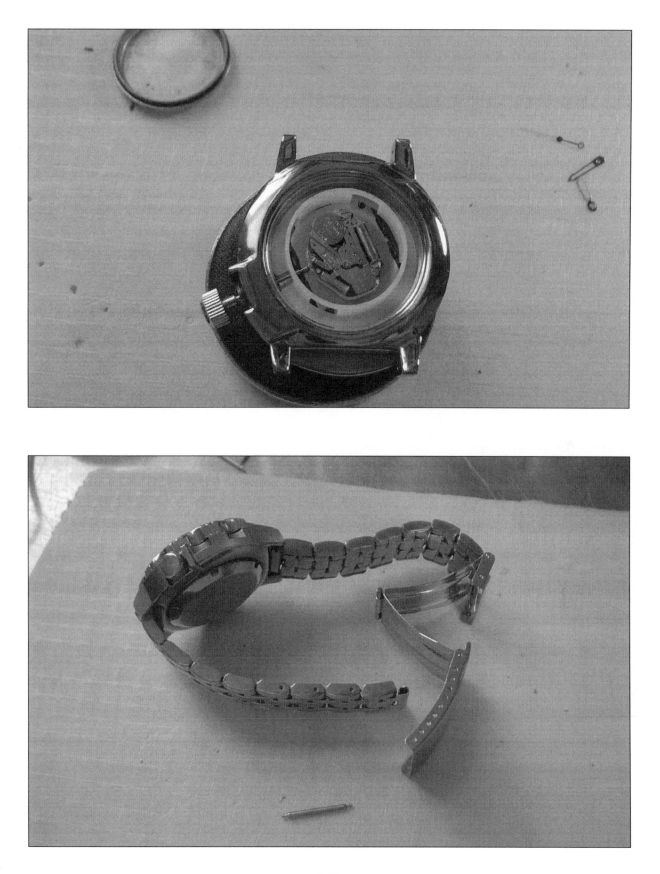

DOWNLOADING THE COLOR EBOOK & VIEWING THE WEBSITE UPDATES

Be sure to check out this link every so often for new updates and also to download the full color PDF ebook, which you can view on your computer or smart phone.

Please type this link in your internet browser for updates:

http://snotboards.com/watch2024.html

8239948R00165

Printed in Germany
by Amazon Distribution
GmbH, Leipzig